# BUREAUCRACY AND ECONOMIC DEVELOPMENT

# BUREAUCRACY AND ECONOMIC DEVELOPMENT

R.K. Panda
K.C. Patnaik

ABHIJEET PUBLICATIONS
Delhi 110 094

**ABHIJEET PUBLICATIONS**
2/46 Tukhmeerpur Extension
Delhi-110 094
Phone: 011-22960492, 65698474
E-mail: abhijeetpublication@gmail.com

BUREAUCRACY AND ECONOMIC DEVELOPMENT

*First Published 2010*

ISBN 978-93-80031-59-0



PRINTED IN INDIA

Published by J.K. Singh for Abhijeet Publications, Delhi-110 094, Lasertypeset by Gaurav Graphics, New Delhi and Printed at Himanshu Printers, Delhi.

# Preface

In recent years, there is considerable academic discourse regarding the efficiency of the bureaucracy on one hand and the benefits emanating from democratization of governance on the other. This book specializes at the point of intersection of both the directions as outlined. Participatory mode of governance has been introduced in multiplicity of the development schemes which have been introduced in the last two decades or so. In the context of the changed paradigm of economic development, bureaucratic efficiency is generally measured by analyzing the outcome indicators of the development schemes implemented in different parts of Orissa. The analysis depicted in the book is in no way a discrepancy against the general notion. In the course of our data collection, large number of agencies particularly AFC Ltd., Bhubaneswar; District Soil Conservation Department, Nawarangpur (Govt. of Orissa); District Soil Conservation Department, Koraput (Govt. of Orissa); District Divisional Forest Office, Ghumsar South, (Govt. of Orissa); Divisional Forest Office, Berhampur, (Govt. of Orissa) have provided all the relevant information as necessitated in the study. We express our sincere gratitude to all those agencies. We acknowledge the support rendered by the Chief Librarian, Ratan Tata Library, Delhi University for developing the literature in the manuscript. We reveal our profound sense of gratitude to Prof N.B. Pradhan (Retd.), Berhampur University for his intellectual support while preparing the manuscript. We thank Dr C.R. Das, Nabakrushna Choudhury Centre for Development Studies, Bhubaneswar; Prof. Madan Mohan Sahu, ICFAI National College, Berhampur for encouraging us while preparing the manuscript. Dr U.Ch. Panigrahy, Lecturer in Economics of Gopalpur Science College, Gopalpur and Mrs Archana Bhagat, Faculty of ICFAI National College, Berhampur deserve our special thanks for suggesting changes required in the manuscript. A cross section of beneficiaries of the different development schemes which are considered in this book has spared their invaluable time for giving us unbiased information. They deserve special thanks. Last but not least, we acknowledge Abhijeet Publications, Delhi for gladly accepting the manuscript for publication of this book.

**Authors**

# Contents

# 1

# Introduction

## 1.1 Background

Bureaucracy is a concept in sociology and political science referring to the way that the administrative execution and enforcement of legal rules is socially organized. This office organization is characterized by standardized procedure, formal division of responsibility, hierarchy, and impersonal social relationships (from *New World Encyclopedia*). Bureaucracy is derived from the word bureau, used from the early eighteenth century in Western Europe to refer not only to a writing desk, but to an office, or a workplace, where officials worked. The original French meaning of the word *bureau* was the *baize* used to cover desks. The Greek suffix *kratia* or *kratos* means "power" or "rule". Bureaucracy thus basically means office power or office rule, the rule of the officialdom. The term bureaucracy came into use shortly before the French Revolution of 1789, and from there spread rapidly to other countries. Max Weber (1947) has been one of the most influential user of the term bureaucracy in its social science sense. He is well-known for his study of bureaucratization of society, and many aspects of modern public administration go back to him. A classic, hierarchically organized civil service of the continental type is—if basically mistakenly—called "Weberian civil service". Weber described the "ideal type" bureaucracy in positive terms, considering it to be a more rational and efficient form of organization than the alternatives that preceded it, which he characterized as "charismatic domination" and "traditional domination." According to his terminology, bureaucracy is part of legal domination. However, he also emphasized that bureaucracy becomes inefficient when a decision must be adapted to an individual case. According to Weber, the attributes of modern bureaucracy include its impersonality, concentration of the means of administration, a leveling effect on social and economic differences, and implementation of a system of authority that is practically indestructible. Thus, bureaucracy goes beyond division of labor in a broad sense, although that is a necessary condition for the existence of bureaucratic systems.

The bureaucracy not only implements governmental policies but also helps to shape them. The bureaucracy is a major base of power that can be difficult to control. Max Weber described the bureaucracy as a "rational" way for society to organize itself; they are found not only in government but throughout society. Weber believed that bureaucracies shared certain characteristics:

- *Chain of Command:* A form of organization characterized by a hierarchical structure of authority.
- *Division of Labor:* Work divided among specialized workers in order to improve productivity.
- *Impersonality:* Persons are treated on "merit" principles, all "clients" served are treated equally according to rules; records are maintained to assure that rules are followed.

Advances in technology and the increasing size and complexity of society have contributed to the growth of bureaucratic power. In Karl Marx's theory of historical materialism, the historical origin of bureaucracy is to be found in four sources: religion, the formation of the state, commerce, and technology. According to Marx's analysis, the earliest bureaucracies consisted of castes of religious clergy, officials, and scribes operating various rituals, and armed functionaries specifically delegated to keep order. In the historical transition from primitive egalitarian communities to a civil society divided into social classes and estates, occurring from about 10,000 years ago, authority is increasingly centralized in, and enforced by, a state apparatus existing separately from society. This state formulates, imposes and enforces laws, and levies taxes, giving rise to an officialdom enacting these functions. But the growth of trade and commerce adds a new, distinctive dimension to bureaucracy, insofar as it requires the keeping of accounts and the processing/recording of transactions, as well as the enforcement of legal rules governing trade. A fourth source of bureaucracy inherent in the technologies of mass production, which require many standardized routines and procedures to be performed. This type of bureaucracy is nowadays often called a technocracy, which owes its power to control over specialized technical knowledge.

In Marx's theory, bureaucracy rarely creates new wealth by itself, but rather controls, coordinates, and governs the production, distribution, and consumption of wealth. The bureaucracy as a social stratum derives its income from the appropriation of part of the social surplus product of human labor. Wealth is appropriated by the bureaucracy by law through fees, taxes, levies, tributes, licensing etc. Bureaucracy is therefore always a "cost" to society, but this cost may be accepted insofar as it makes social order possible, and maintains it.

Michel Crozier wrote *The Bureaucratic Phenomenon* (1964) as a re-examination of Weber's (1922) concept of the efficient ideal bureaucracy in the light of the way that bureaucratic organizations had actually developed. Where as for Weber, bureaucracy was the ultimate expression of a trend toward the efficient, rational organization, Crozier examined bureaucracy as a form of organization that evokes: "... the slowness, the ponderousness, the routine, the complication of procedures and the maladapted responses of the bureaucratic organization to the needs which they should satisfy" (Crozier, 1964). The analysis of bureaucracy by the Austrian school reflects its characteristic focus on economics, and emphasizes the distinction between bureaucratic management and profit management.

Bureaucratic organizations are at the center of Communist political systems. In redistributive socialist economies, bureaucrats play a central role in the administration and allocation of resources from public property and the implementation of state policies at the local level (Szelenyi 1978). With the transition experienced by former communist countries from a centrally planned economy to one increasingly dominated by market forces and new institutional rules, the bureaucratic apparatus has not diminished in importance. Bureaucrats bred in the old system still dominate the governing structure of these societies and have adapted to the new rules of incipient markets (Ivan Szelényi and Robert Manchin 1987).

Public bureaucracies play a key role in the process of nation building, socio-economic development, policy formulation and policy implementation, especially in the context of the developing societies. The maintenance of National integrity and the success and failures of various programs of socio-economic development in these countries have depended to a considerable extent on the capacities of these bureaucracies.

## 1.2 Bureaucracy in India

The bureaucracy in India is the product of two different sets of influences: British traditions of the past and the democratic welfare state of the present. The bureaucracy, created by the British to maintain the imperialist traditions of a colonial Government was a remarkable administrative legacy. However, since the end of the colonial period it has been persistently argued that Indian administrators, retaining negative aspects of the imperial legacy are maladjusted, lack dedication and tend to be authoritarian. In India, bureaucratic dysfunction has become a norm. The Indian bureaucracy suffers from certain strange paradoxes. A rigid adherence to procedure combined with a ready susceptibility to personal pressure and intervention.

One of the most undesirable characteristics of bureaucracy in India is that administration is treated as a secret even as esoteric process. There is no appreciation of the citizens view point and exercises in public relations are aimed more at publicity and propaganda than at establishing rapport with the community or making genuine attempts to improve the public in the administrative process. The bureaucracy in India is so rigidly hierarchical that there is no mutual trust between Government units or even employees with in a particular department. When confronted with a difficult decision. The Indian bureaucrat seldom makes any attempt to tackle the problem with initiative and imagination.

The administrative and management culture prevalent in India today reflects the family atmosphere and the way people live at home. This rigid nature of ties in the family is reflected in the control that people adopt at the office. People are actually taught not to question but only to remember and follow. The superiors expect loyalty not to the project but to him. Corruption has almost become the way of life. A sort of cynicism seems to prevail that one has got to live with it. The officers' excessive dependence upon notations entered by the junior clerks on every file, the outdated administrative procedures and formalism, the excessive delay in forwarding an application, the infinite time taken to pass the final order, the uncertainty and variance in the application of rules and regulations, methods of flattery that encourage subservience for obtaining service, from the administrators and the, lubrication required in the form of payment to powerful political or bureaucratic functionaries to get the work done have all become a part of the administrative culture of India. Performance is at the level of the lowest common denominator.

Apart from its relations with the political leadership, the other factor which, influences the administrative culture of India is lack of morality in the administration, unethical conduct is not only responsible for carelessness and irresponsibility towards citizens. The prevailing political atmosphere, the falling standards of public life and the loss of moral values among the political leaders have bred a corresponding insensitivity, demoralization and unresponsiveness among public officials.

To make the matter worse the Indian Administrative

Service (IAS) created after independence came to exist with the (ICS) and initiated all the valuable acquisitions of the later. The IAS also accepted the same legacies of the ICS including its claim to exclusiveness and class consciousness. The changing role of India bureaucracy is the major issue of our times, commenting on the role, T.N. Chaturvedi( ) writes, "The Civil Service has to undergo radical structural, procedural and attitudinal changes if it has to serve as an effective instrument of change and progress in a developing society. The civil service has to cultivate much wider social awareness and responsiveness as well as social base apart from the traditional virtues of integrity, functional efficiency and a sense of fair play and impartiality."

With the establishment of democracy after independence, the Indian masses began to be politicized and conscious of their own rights. As a result of government initiative and programmes, the social structure and values also gradually began to undergo changes. The universal adult franchise and agri industrial development has changed the basic Indian philosophy, a philosophy under which the people are expected to obey the government (Bhambhri, 1971). The bureaucracy has now come to function among the people who are conscious of their right and who not only obey but also make demands upon the administration. The new administrative system of India emphasizes "a public not parasitic in its relationship to the administrative system, but participant, a public which accepted duties as well as made demands, a public confident in administrative hierarchy and motivated to share in the responsibilities of development" (Eldersveld, et al 1968).

Thus, under the new setup, the area of bureaucratic functioning has enlarged both quantitatively and qualitatively. Its function is no longer limited to the maintenance of law and order. It has now to undertake vast complex tasks of nation building and socio-economic development. But what role does the bureaucracy actually play in this task of nation building and socio-economic development? But a large body of critiques including Administrative Reforms Commission and similar Commissions in the states provide a very much gloomy picture on the efficacy of bureaucratic functioning in India. All these critiques do indicate that the bureaucracy has failed in its task of nation building and socio-economic change of the people. Over the years, there has been an increase in corruption and inefficiency in the bureaucracy; its independence, integrity and devotion to public interest have also been undermined. It is now widely recognized that such a bureaucracy is ill-equipped for the massive and complex tasks of nation building and socio-economic development.

But why has the bureaucracy failed in its task of nation building and socio-economic development. In the present study we propose to examine this question with particular reference to the Bureaucratic Functioning in Orissa.

## Need of the Study

During the last twenty years economists are found to be more concerned about investigating the political behavior. Discarding the naïve view that the public sector functions to promote the social welfare and further the public interest economists have begun to examine the behaviour of utility maximising politicians, voters and bureaucrats. It is focused upon the nature of incentives and constraints which each group faces in an attempt to trace out the behavioural patterns implied by utility maximization within a given environment. The new approach to the study of political economy grows out 'the public choice school' founded by James Buchanan at the Virginia Polytechnique Institute. Rather than taking the existing set of fiscal institutions as given, theory must be of public sector it is necessary for the economists to turn attention to the dynamics of non market decision making. The greater proportion of the economics literature has concentrated attention upon the working of the market system, public sector economies have traditionally been studied by examining the impact of tax, subsidies and public expenditure upon market prices. The public choice approach examines the internal operation of the public sector itself. That is, it focuses attention on the institutions of the public sector and the decision making process and distribution of public services and the means of financing them. Whilst the public choice school has concentrated attention upon collective choice mechanism (such as voting system), through which the demands of individual voters are engaged into a single collective preference. It is only comparatively recently that the supply side of the equation (i.e. Bureaucracy) has been subject to critical analysis.

Today there is increasing concern about complex organizations, especially about the depersonalization associated with them, their unresponsiveness to social needs, the nature of resources allocation within them and the power that they reveal to the society. One such set of complex organizations is the public sector bureaucracy. As the public sector grows in size relative to the rest of the economy, more and more activity is organized within the bureaucracy. None of the nation's wealth is allocated and distributed through decision taken within the bureaucracy.

## Bureaucracy, Resource Allocation and Political Economy

The subject of economics has often been described as an examination of the allocation of individually owned scarce resources. A considerable part of economic analysis, indeed the bulk of it deals with the price mechanism or market system in solving the problems of production and allocation of resources among the members of the society. The political process however also produces and distributes the products of jointly owned scarce resources. Thus, alongside the market process of the political system there are many different institutional forms for the allocation and distribution of resources. These include: (a) the market and price system; (b) voting procedures; (c) bidding; (d) bargaining; (e) allocation of higher authority, fiat or dictatorship; (f) allocation by the custom, including gifts and inheritance; (g) allocation by chance. Economists, however, have built up a grand theory of price mechanism and have until, comparatively recently ignored the importance of non market system, including the political process of voting and bureaucracy. One of the most popular institutional/political economists is J.K. Galbraith ( ) divides the economy into public system and market system in his famous work "Economics and Public

Purpose". The planning system refers to the internal planning by individual firms and organisations which although influenced by market signals, does not take place within a market context.

One of the features of modern industrial societies is the capital intensive nature of the production process, the size of industrial organization and has the relative importance of planning system over the market system. The planning system is served by the 'technostructure' like group of managers, lawyers, scientists, etc. who control the activities of the large scale organisations and Multi National Companies. The technostructure exists to influence consumers in the market place and to obtain long term government contracts. Resources are not allocated via competitive markets, but are instead allocated by bargains struck between the various groups the various groups within the corporations and government purchasers. Examination of the nature of the bargaining and exchange process which takes place in non market institutions has resulted in the reemergence of political economy.

In recent years partly because of the failure of the Keynesian macro-economic demand management, economic policy makers have turned to what has come to be referred as Supply Side Economics. Low productivity, poor competitiveness (both at home and abroad), low rate of economic growth and industrial relations have deep rooted causes in the structural and institutional dimension of the economy (i.e. its supply side). In order to deal with the issues economists need to turn their attention to organizational process and non economic factors.

## 1.4 Growth of Public Sector and Bureaucracy

Public sector employment has been growing in the major industrial countries during the post war period. This growth in the public sector of Organisation of Economic Cooperation and Development (OECD) countries is accounted for in a number of ways. Demographic changes in population, especially increased incidense of literate people, employment option for even the retire people have caused public employment to rise. Expansion in the welfare state along with an increase in the scope of the regulatory role of government (i.e. Environmental and Consumer Protection) has resulted in an increase in the number of public sector employees.

A large public sector relative to the market or private sector of the economy has important consequences. Not only does the financing of public sector activities through taxes and borrowing have an impact upon market prices and allocations, but a large proportion of the nation,s resources are allocated and distributed by non market means through bureaucracy. The economic analysis of bureaucracy is an examination of these allocative decisions and processes. How do bureaucrats make decisions, whose interest do they serve; what are the consequences of bureaucratic decisions, are public bureaucrats compared with corporate bureaucracy in the private sector; how effective is the public's control over bureaucracies and what are the limits of bureaucracy's power to implement the policies that will bring about the new society? These are the principal questions which have been considered throughout the study.

## 1.5 Objectives of the Study

Orissa comprising 4.74 percent of India's landmass and with 31.66 million people (1991 census) accounts for 3.74 percent of the population of the country. Nearly 87 percent of its population lives in the rural areas and depend mostly on agriculture for their livelihood. The state has good resources of minerals including precious and semi precious stones. It has also abundant water resources and mineral resources. Planned exploitation and optimum utilisation of rich mineral, land, water and other resources including human resources holds the key to rapid economic development of the state.

Despite vast natural resources and human resources and substantial progress achieved during the last 58 years of planned development, Orissa continues to be a less developed state with high incidence of poverty. High dependence on and low productivity of the primary sector have resulted in significant fluctuations in the growth rate from year to year.

In a democratic setup, three groups of people viz: politicians, Bureaucracy and voters are responsible for the economic development of their geographical region. For last several years, it is continuously observed that Orissa politics is filled with the persons who lack leadership quality and dedication due to variety of factors. The significant majority of voters in Orissa are illiterate and they are not aware of the weight of their votes which ultimately determines the development potential of the state. The private investors mostly the multinational corporations are interested in quick disposal of government clearance to their projects. The bureaucracy has to play a very dynamic role here and act with foresight to satisfy the private partners in the process of economic development.

## 1.6 Hypotheses

1. The bureaucrats through their dynamic role and effective delivery system can maximize the regional economic development and even gratify the private partners in the process of economic development.
2. The performances of bureaucrats with regard to development is better where there is participatory development mode.
3. There is bureaucratic inefficiency where there is no participatory development.

## 1.7 Study Approach and Methodology

### *Methodology*

This study uses both qualitative and quantitative tools to undertake a comprehensive and Preliminary inter-sectoral appraisal, through State level macro and micro-analysis. The Methodology seeks to generate necessary information that enables an independent review of the effects and impacts of development policies and programmes on rural poverty in Orissa. Rather than using traditional methods of large-scale sampling design that can be amenable to statistical analysis, this research applies a combination of case study and quantitative macro analysis methods that deepen our understanding of the constraints and challenges to development in the state. We have tried to highlight emerging issues in rural poverty at the state and field level, as well as policy and operational constraints. This study has analyzed extensive secondary information; both unpublished and published; related to development policy, project formulation and implementation. The study also is based on selected case studies to assess policy effects within relevant sectors. For examining agricultural change, the study undertook a case study at Kashipur Block in Rayagada district where Integrated Wasteland Development Programme has been implemented. To examine the micro finance led development programme, the micro finance activity in selected villages of Nawarangpur district has been analysed. To understand the pattern of participatory development towards attaining Sustainable Rural development 14 Joint Forest Management (JFM) villages in Ganjam District have been covered. This research also attempted to examine the costs and benefits connected to livelihood generation, and ecological sustainability of the forests. Similarly in the event of absence of participatory development, the poverty reducing impacts of Public distribution System has been analysed and on the basis of such a case study, this research has made an attempt to examine issues of food security and hunger. The present work has adopted both theoretical and empirical approach to achieve the objectives. Theoretically, different published sources like authentic books and referred journals have been studied to arrive at a suitable model on the functioning of bureaucracy. The empirical content of this study is analyzed on the basis of micro studies obtained from a cross section of respondents for various mentioned cases using questionnaire method. As the study requires various types of cases, thus, the sample size, study Area, Reference Period, Statistical techniques and statistical tools vary from cases to case. The details of these methodological aspects are mentioned in the respective chapters where the case is explained.

## 1.8 Limitations

1. The work involves a lot of qualitative variables and

thus poses the obvious difficulty in quantifying them. We contemplate to use suitable methodology for this, which is likely to be not unique in character.

2. The regional variation in the attitude of bureaucracy can't be inserted into the model due to difficulty in covering a broader area.
3. Instead of obtaining information from the bureaucrats directly, the study has introduced the concept of measuring rural development under different categories of schemes as mentioned in the methodology part. It has been viewed that the outcome indicators of the developmental interventions made by the bureaucrats could provide a true picture of bureaucrat led development.
4. The aspects like bureaucratic corruption, without which development would be more strengthened has not been considered because of the non accessibility of information.

## 1.9 Chapterization

Chapter-1: Introduction

Chapter-2: Theory of Bureaucracy

Chapter-3: The Bureaucracy in India

Chapter-4: Status of Economic Development in Orissa

Chapter-5: Role of Bureaucracy in Economic Development: A Case Study of Watershed Programme and Joint Forest Management programme

Chapter-6: Role of Bureaucracy in Economic Development: A Case Study of Micro Finance and Public Distribution System in Orissa

Chapter-7: Concluding Remarks and Suggestions.

# 2

# Theory of Bureaucracy

The emergence and growth of bureaucracy over the last two hundred years has been the subject of considerable discussion among social scientists. Conventional, bourgeois sociology argues that bureaucratic hierarchies are an unavoidable feature of modern societies, whose size and complexity preclude any possibility of popular democratic control over political, economic and social life.

Weber believed that the requirements of the Industrial Age necessitated the use in public sector management of bureaucratic or highly centralized, rule bound, expert-driven hierarchic systems. That system as it has evolved lent itself to excesses and has proved to be inadequate to meet the needs of the Information Age. Various experiments are underway to reorient public administration to make it more flexible, efficient and responsive so that it may better serve the public interest in the Information Age. However, it is by no means clear that this process of reform will lead to more enlightened or effective government. On the contrary, it may produce a system of public management which represents a more pervasively intrusive, impersonal and oppressive form of government than anything. In that sense his insights were prophetic and are relevant today. Weber's writings on power relationships in society, the sources of legitimacy of state power and its organization and administration do not fit neatly within the epistemology of modern cultural theorists. Max Weber saw bureaucracy as the most rational and effective mode of organizing the activities of large number of people because it ensured decision-making according to general rules rather than the whims of officials, cultivated trained "experts", and reduced the possibilities of corruption and nepotism (Baron & Diedrof 1813). Robert Michels (1970) extended Weber's theory of bureaucracy, originally developed to analyze the officialdom of the capitalist state, to the study of the mass working class parties and unions of the early twentieth century (Engels--). The "iron law of oligarchy", today embraced by social-democrats and neo-Stalinists, purports that the growth and usurpation of power by a layer of full-time officials are inevitable features of mass working class parties and unions under capitalism and of any post-capitalist social order.

Ernest Mandel's work provides a powerful Marxian alternative to the Stalinist, social-democratic and bourgeois theories that deny the possibility of democratically organized workers' struggles and workers' power in the modern world. In a series of works, Mandel (1992) presented a complex, coherent and empirically well grounded response to the notion that the arrogation of power by a minority of officials and experts is the "inevitable" result of complex, large-scale, modern social organization. Mandel argued that bureaucracy is the product of specific, historically limited relations among human beings and between human beings and the natural world of specific social relations and material forces of production. Mandel's theory of bureaucracy provides a contemporary defence, extension and deepening of the classical Marxist discussion of bureaucracy, in particular the work of Rosa Luxemburg and Leon Trotsky.

For Mandel, the emergence of bureaucracies in both the mass working class parties and unions under capitalism and in the post-capitalist societies is rooted in the reproduction of the social division of labour between mental-supervisory and manual labour. Whether the product of the episodic character of working class struggle under capitalism, or profound material scarcity in the case of twentieth century post-revolutionary societies, the persistent division between "head" work and "hand" work gives rise to a layer of full-time officials who administer either mass parties and unions or the post-capitalist state apparatus. This layer, in most circumstances, evolves into a distinct social layer with its own material interests, politics, and ideology. The development of the bureaucracy does not enhance the "efficiency" and effectivity of mass workers organizations under capitalism or of centrally planned economic life in the post-capitalist societies. Instead, the officialdom's monopoly of power undermines the ability of the working class to either defend its most immediate interests under capitalism or to build a viable alternative to capitalism. Mandel's theory of bureaucracy is one of the central scientific foundations of the revolutionary political project of working class self-activity, self-organization and self-emancipation.

Our discussion of Mandel's theory of bureaucracy is divided into three parts. In the first, we will examine Mandel's analysis of the origin and role of the labour bureaucracy in the capitalist social formations, and his theory of the revolutionary workers' organization as an alternative to bureaucratic reformism. We will also assess Mandel's attempt to explain why, contrary to the expectation of revolutionary Marxists, no truly mass revolutionary parties have emerged in the advanced capitalist countries since the 1920s. In the second part, we will review Mandel's attempt to update and refine Trotsky's analysis of the bureaucracy in the post-capitalist societies. Specifically we will grapple with the issue of whether the bureaucracy's relationship with the working class constitutes a new mode of production, and whether these regimes can be understood as "workers' states" in any meaningful, Marxian sense. We will conclude with a discussion of the political importance of Mandel's theory of bureaucracy.

## I. The Labour Bureaucracy in the Capitalist Social Formations

The classical Marxist discussion of the labour bureaucracy began as an attempt to explain the growth of reformism within the mass socialist parties of the early twentieth century. The leaders of the revolutionary left-wing of European socialism did not merely criticize the theory and practice of the mainstream of social-democracy, but attempted to uncover the social and material roots of the labour movements' conservatism and ultimate capitulation to their national capitalist classes during the First World War Given the practical revolutionary success of the Bolsheviks, it was not surprising that Lenin's thesis on the degeneration of social democracy became, in Mandel's words, "the 'dogma' for revolutionary Marxists for nearly half a century" (Woodrow, 1887). According to Lenin, the growth of reformism in the labour movement in the advanced capitalist countries was the ideological expression of the "labour aristocracy," a privileged minority of the western working class whose superior standard of living came from a share of the "super profits" extracted by the imperialist bourgeoisie in the colonies and semi-colonies. This layer of workers supported the "petty-bourgeois intellectuals" in the party and union apparatus who propagated reformist and "social patriotic" politics before and during World War I. (Ludwig, 1944)

Mandel was the first thinker in the revolutionary Marxist tradition to reject explicitly Lenin's notion of the "labour aristocracy." Mandel cites three important reasons for jettisoning the notion that a layer of workers in the imperialist countries share in the "super-profits" extracted from workers in the "third world." First, the multinational corporations' total profits from their direct investments in Africa, Asia and Latin America can not account for the wage bill of even the most well paid, unionized workers in the industrialized countries. Put simply, workers in the "third world" do not produce sufficient surplus value to "bribe" a significant sector of the working class in the Europe, the US or Japan. Second, the gap between the wages of workers in the "north" and "south" is much greater than wage differentials among workers in the "north." In other words, the entire working classes of Europe, the US and Japan are potential "labour aristocracies." But, Mandel points out, these global wage differentials are the result of the greater capital intensity (organic composition of capital) and higher productivity of labour (rate of surplus value) in the advanced capitalist social formations, not some sharing of "super profits" between capital and labour in the industrialized countries. Put simply, the better paid workers of the "north" are more exploited than the poorly paid workers of the "south". Finally, Mandel points out that some of the best paid workers in Europe, the U.S. and Japan, especially those in the metal working industries, were among the most militant and radical proletarians, providing the mass base of the revolutionary Communist parties of the 1920s and early 1930s (Iowi, 1979).

Mandel found a more fruitful Marxian discussion of the labour bureaucracy under capitalism in the work of Rosa Luxemburg (Scholz & Wood, 1988). Luxemburg, well before either Lenin or Trotsky, understood that the emergence and development of the trade union and party officialdom was the key to German social-democracy's growing conservatism (Huber & Shipan, 2002). In the wake of the Russian revolution of 1905, Luxemburg encountered opposition to her advocacy of the "mass strike" as a tactic for the German workers' movement from both the openly "revisionist" wing of the SPD led by Bernstein, and from the "orthodox Marxist" leadership of the party around Kautsky and Bebel. She concluded that the full-time party and union officials' hegemony over the SPD, not simply the influence of middle class intellectuals, was the root of the entire leadership's refusal to countenance any activities other than election campaigns and routinized collective bargaining. For Luxemburg, this bureaucracy, once consolidated in the mass working class institutions, placed greater importance upon the preservation of the party and union apparatus than on any attempt to deepen and extend the workers' struggles.

Mandel located the origins of the labour bureaucracy in the episodic and discontinuous character of working class struggle under capitalism. For Mandel, the necessary condition for the development of class consciousness is the self-activity and self-organization of the workers themselves. It is the experience of mass, collective and successful struggles against capital and its state in the work place and the community that opens layers of workers to radical and revolutionary political ideas. When workers do not engage in mass struggle or suffer defeats, they become open to conservative and reactionary ideas as one section of the class makes a futile attempt to defend their particular sectional (national, occupational, racial-ethnic, gender) interests against other sectors of the working class. In sum, it is the level of class militancy and independence, not cultural influences like suburbanization, television, films and the like, that determines the basic parameters of class consciousness under capitalism (Ramseyer and Rosenbluth, 1993).

The working class cannot be, as whole, permanently active in the class struggle. The entire working class cannot consistently engage in strikes, demonstrations and other forms of political activity because this class is separated from effective possession of the means of production and is compelled to sell their labour power to capital in order to survive. The "actually existing" working class can only engage in mass struggles as a class in extraordinary, revolutionary or pre-revolutionary situations, which, because of the structural position of wage labour under capitalism, must be of short duration. Most of the time, different segments of the working class become active in the struggle against capitalism at different times.

In the wake of successful mass struggles, only a minority of the workers remain consistently active. Most of this "workers' vanguard"—the layer of workers who "even during a lull in the struggle...does not abandon the front lines of the class struggle but continues the war, so to speak, 'by other means'" preserves and transmits to newer workers the traditions of mass struggle in the workplace or the community (McCubbins and Rosenbluth, 1993). However, a minority of this "militant minority", together with middle class intellectuals who have access to cultural skills from which the bulk of the working class is excluded, must take on responsibility for administering the unions or political parties created by periodic upsurges of mass activity. Mandel recognized that "the development of mass political or trade-union organizations is inconceivable without an apparatus of full-timers and functionaries." However, he points out that the emergence of a layer of full time officials brings with it the risk that working-class organizations will themselves become divided between layers exercising different functions. Specialization can result in a growing monopoly of knowledge, of centralized information. Knowledge is power, and a monopoly of it leads to power over people... if not checked, [this can-CP] mean a real division between new bosses and the bossed-over mass (Chowdhury, 2006).

During the unavoidable lulls in the class struggle, when the vast majority of the working class is passive, the potential for bureaucratization is actualized. Especially during "long-waves" of capitalist growth, when most workers' living standards and working conditions improve without tumultuous, mass struggles, the officialdom of the mass workers' organizations can separate themselves from the rest of the working class. Those workers who become officials of the unions and political parties begin to experience conditions of life very different from those who remain in the workplace. The new officials find themselves freed from the daily humiliations of the capitalist labour process. They are no longer subject to either deskilled and alienated labor or the petty-despotism of supervisors. Able to set their own hours, plan and direct their own activities, and devote the bulk of their working hours to "fighting for the workers", the officials seek to consolidate these privileges and create new ones, in particular incomes substantially higher than those of the workers they purportedly represent. In defence of their privileges, which become quite substantial as the unions and mass working class parties gain a place in bourgeois society, the labor bureaucracy excludes rank and file activists in the unions and parties from any real decision making power.

The consolidation of the labor bureaucracy as a social layer distinct and separate from the rest of the working class under capitalism gives rise to its distinctive political practice and world-view. The preservation of the apparatus of the mass union or party, as an end itself, becomes the main objective of the labor bureaucracy. The labor bureaucrats seek to contain working class militancy within boundaries that do not threaten the continued existence of the institutions which are the basis of the officials' unique life style. Thus the "dialectic of partial conquests", the possibility that new struggles may result in the destruction of the mass organizations of the working class, buttress the labor bureaucracy's reliance on electoral campaigns and parliamentary pressure tactics ("lobbying') to win political reforms, and strictly regimented collective bargaining to increase wages and improve working conditions. Any and all discussion, no less attempts to promote the tumultuous self-activity and self-organization of working and oppressed people in the forms of militant workplace actions, mass political strikes or the like, must be quashed (Draper, 1979). At this point, the bureaucracy's organizational fetishism (giving priority the survival of the apparatus over new advances in the struggle) grows into a substitutionism that demands the workers' unquestioning obedience to leaders who claim that they know what is the best for the workers.

As Mandel never tired of pointing out, the reformist substitution of electoral politics and routinized bargaining for mass struggles ignores "the structural character of the basic relations of production and of political and social class power." In other words, the politics of the labor bureaucracies in the capitalist social formations are utopian in the most negative sense of the word (Mandal, 1992). The labor bureaucracies' attempts to broker the struggle between capital and labor, modifying very gradually the relationship of forces in favor of the workers constantly flounders on capitalism's unavoidable crises of profitability and the resulting intensification of the class struggle. The history of both the classical social-democratic parties and the Communist parties after 1935, when they began their transformation into reformist parties, sadly confirms the thoroughly unrealistic character of the bureaucracy's gradualism. During revolutionary and pre-revolutionary crises, like those in Italy in 1920, Germany during 1918-1923, Spain and France in 1936-37, and Chile in 1970-73, the social-democratic and Stalinist parties successfully disorganized the workers' struggles and organizations (workers' councils, factory committees and the like) in the name of preserving bourgeois democracy and the past conquests of the workers' movement. Unfortunately, the derailing of mass revolutionary struggles did not merely waste opportunities to seize state power and begin the construction of a new democratic and socialist order, but opened the road to the forces of reaction. The Italian Fascists' victory in 1921, the Nazi's seizure of power in 1933, Franco's military victory in 1939, the collapse of the French Third Republic in 1940, and Pinochet's coup of September 11, 1973 were all the products of the working class' inability to seize power when the opportunity presented itself. In sum, the labor bureaucracy's attempt to "self-limit" the workers' struggles within the boundaries of capitalist democracy facilitated the consolidation of dictatorial and repressive forms of capitalist rule (Garston, 1993).

The reformist substitution of electoral campaigns, parliamentary pressure politics and bureaucratized collective bargaining for working class and popular mass action has led to profound disorganization and passivity in the ranks of the labor movement in the west since the Second World War. While such bureaucratic forms of "struggle" were able to "deliver the goods" in the form of higher wages, improved benefits, stabilized working conditions and an expanding "welfare state" during the "long wave" of expansion of the 1950s and 1960s, this strategy proved completely inadequate during the "long wave" of stagnation that began in the late 1960s. As the crisis of capitalist profitability deepened, reformism's substitutionism gave way to realpolitik - adapting to the new "reality" of declining living and working conditions.

In the present-day social-democratic System, governments can redistribute the capitalist produce for reducing inequality and injustice What if there is no economic growth at all as a result of capitalist crisis? The gradualists can then only repeat mechanically: there is no alternative; there is no way out (Chowdhury, 2006).

Eschewing militancy and direct action by workers and other oppressed people, the labor bureaucracy and reformist politicians in the west have no choice but to make concessions to the employers' offensive and to administer capitalist state austerity. The spectacle of reformist bureaucrats shunning the struggle for reforms has been repeated across the capitalist world in the last two decades with tragic results: from the Italian Communist party's embrace of austerity, to the concession bargaining of the US AFL-CIO officials, to the Mitterand regimes' budget cuts, privatization and deregulation, to the subjugation of an ANC-COSATU led government in post-apartheid South Africa to what some have called the "sado-monetarism" of the IMF and World Bank. Again, even the most moderate forms of social-democratic gradualism prove to be profoundly utopian-unable to defend the workers' past gains no less win significant new reforms during the crisis of capitalist profitability (Draper, 1979).

Given its roots in the necessarily episodic character of mass struggle under capitalism, is the bureaucratization of the mass organizations of the working class inevitable? Clearly, Mandel's theory of the labor bureaucracy in the capitalist social formations lead us to the conclusion that reformism will continue to be a problem in the workers' movement until capitalism is overthrown internationally. However, Mandel's theory also identifies countervailing social forces to, and safeguards against the bureaucratization of the political parties and trade unions. In perhaps his greatest political-theoretical contribution, his elaboration and clarification of the Leninist theory of organization, Mandel demonstrates how the same episodic process of class struggle that creates the environment for the growth of the labor bureaucracy provides the human material for a mass, revolutionary workers' party. Out of the ebbs and flows of the class struggle, a workers vanguard is precipitated. The ability of a revolutionary socialist nucleus to organize and eventually fuse with the most active, militant and radical workers create a variety of potential counter-weights to the labor bureaucracy.

In non-revolutionary periods, non-socialist organizations of "advanced workers" in organized and unorganized workplaces—what in the US we call "rank and file' currents—play an important role in keeping alive traditions of militancy and solidarity in the workers' movements and fighting for effective, democratic safeguards (election of officials, reduction of salaries, free debate and discussion of competing positions, etc.) in the unions and popular organizations. Often such organizations are able to displace the party and union bureaucracies and lead important successful day-to-day struggles that develop the political and ideological self-confidence of the workers. Even in non-revolutionary periods, relatively small revolutionary socialist groups play a crucial role in organizing these "rank and file" currents and in educating the most radical workers in Marxian theory and politics. In revolutionary and pre-revolutionary conjunctures, the effective fusion of revolutionary nuclei with the broad vanguard of the class into a real revolutionary workers party could open the possibility of socialist revolution. A mass revolutionary party with significant roots in the workers' movement can help promote the formation and centralization of organs of working class power (councils in the neighborhoods, workplaces, schools), pose a practical alternative to the reformist bureaucrats' attempts to limit the struggles within limits compatible with capitalist profitability and political power, and lead a successful seizure of power.

In the late 1930s, Trotsky and his supporters believed that the Second World War would lead to a terminal crisis of bureaucratic rule in the USSR and a rapid collapse of the Stalinist Communist parties in capitalist Europe, opening the road to building new, mass revolutionary workers' organizations. Again in the late 1960s and early 1970s, with the beginning of the "long-wave" of economic stagnation and the constant rise of workers struggles across the capitalist world, revolutionary socialists inside and outside expected their relatively small organizations to grow rapidly and become rooted in the insurgent layers of the working class. Ernest Mandel was certainly not immune to the enthusiasm of this period:

> The essential function of the period from 1968 to the present day [c. 1977—CP] has been to allow the far Left to accumulate sufficient forces to enter this revolutionary period with the realistic possibility of winning over the majority of the working class

(Watson, 1980). The revolutionary left's optimism, often bordering on triumphalism, was sorely disappointed as the wave of mass strikes and pre-revolutionary upsurges of the early 1970s turned into the uninterrupted retreat of the working class across the industrialized world in the 1980s and early 1990s. As the capitalist offensive proceeded with few challenges, most of the generation of students and young workers radicalized in the late 1960s and 1970s abandoned revolutionary politics, and the promising revolutionary organizations of the earlier period stagnated or went into decline. It is only in the past year, with the massive and generally successful public sector workers strike in France, the anti-austerity strikes in Canada, and the still fragmented industrial actions like the Dayton autoworkers' strike in the US, that we see the possible beginnings of a new combativity on the part of the working classes of advanced capitalism.

Mandel in the late 1970s offered some tentative explanations for why the upsurge of the late 1960s and early 1970s had not transformed the European revolutionary left into organizations of several tens of thousands of worker revolutionaries. On the one hand, he pointed to what he saw as a temporary disorientation of the new "militant minority" that had arisen in the European labor movement since 1968. The global recession of 1974-75 and the beginnings of the employers' offensive and austerity drive, coinciding with the defeat of the Portuguese Revolution:

> These comrades were well seasoned and experienced in mounting struggles to defend real wages against inflation, but they were not at all prepared for a fight against massive unemployment.

However, Mandel believed that this working class "has now been thrown onto the defensive temporarily" (Garston, 1993). With nearly twenty years of hindsight, it is quite clear that Mandel gravely underestimated the set-back suffered by the European workers' movement.

On the other hand, Mandel was aware of some of the

cumulative effects of the transformation of the Communist parties into reformist organizations in the 1950s and 1960s that happened in the industrially advanced countries at the end of the Second World War, and especially at the end of the Cold War. This sort of anti-capitalist education had continued even during the Popular Front...Today, Social democratic and Stalinist reformism are joining forces to keep the working class a prisoner of bourgeois and petty-bourgeois ideology. But any vision of the class struggle that focused exclusively on this aspect of reality would underestimate the almost structurally anti-capitalist mainsprings inherent in the class struggle during any phase of pronounced instability.

As the "temporary" set-back of the workers' struggles in the late 1970s turned into the prolonged capitalist offensive of the 1980s and 1990s, Mandel's political co-thinkers began to look at more long-term obstacles to the building of mass revolutionary parties in the advanced capitalist countries. In documents adapted at the last three World Congresses of the Fourth International there has been recognition that the 1950s and 1960s saw a profound break in the history of the workers' vanguard. The notion that revolutionaries merely had to win over already militant, anti-capitalist workers from the existing bureaucratized parties has been replaced by a perspective that envisioned a gradual recomposition of the workers' vanguard through new mass defensive struggles (Augustus, 1981).

Mandel's theory of bureaucracy and his analysis of the social and political transformation of the western Communist parties actually hold the key to explaining the virtual disappearance of a massive layer of radical and revolutionary workers. Mandel, following Trotşky, saw the Seventh World Congress of the Communist International as the turning point in the evolution of the Stalinist parties in the advanced capitalist countries (Ahmed, 1980). The "popular front" strategy transformed the Communists parties politically and sociologically. Politically, the Communist Parties adapted the traditional strategy of reformism—the defense of bourgeois democratic institutions as the best guarantors of the "historic gains" of the labor movement. Sociologically, the 'popular front" led to the wholesale integration of the Communist parties into the labor bureaucracies in France, Italy and (in the late 1960s) Spain. In other words, the CPs were transformed from parties of rank and file worker militants who actively organized in their workplaces against both the bureaucrats and the employers, into recruiting grounds for trade union and party functionaries. Combined with the effects of the long-wave of economic expansion in the 1950s and 1960s, the social transformation of the Communist parties all but destroyed the traditions of militancy, solidarity, democracy and anti-capitalist radicalism defended by the mass workers' vanguard since the late nineteenth century. This new situation poses new and difficult tasks for revolutionary Marxists in the west. While continuing revolutionary socialist propaganda and education aimed at recruiting and training workers activists as Marxists, they must also play an active and leading role in reorganizing a workers' vanguard, around a "class struggle", but not explicitly socialist, program of militancy, solidarity, democracy and political independence (Ahmed 1975).

## II. The Bureaucracy in the Post-Capitalist Societies

Mandel's theory of the Ṣtalinist bureaucracies in the post-capitalist societies deepened Trotsky's pathbreaking Marxist analysis of the origins and contradictions of the bureaucratic rule of the Soviet Union (Alogun, 1983). The bulk of the Bolshevik leaders in the 1920s viewed the growth of the full-time officialdom in the post-revolutionary party and state, in Mandel's words, "as a purely power-political, institutional... administrative problem" because of their "substitutionist concept of the party-worker relationship: the dictatorship of the proletariat is exercised by the party under the leadership of its Leninist Central Committee." In other words, most Russian revolutionaries saw the problem as one of "bureaucratism"—inefficient administration and bad-decision making by incompetent officials. In 1923, Trotsky was the first Marxist to understand and develop both a rigorous Marxian analysis of the dynamics and contradictions of the bureaucratized Soviet society, and a consistent political strategy, based on the revolutionary self-organization and self-activity of the workers, to oppose bureaucratic rule (Barkam and Okumu 1979).

Mandel and Trotsky's theory of the bureaucratization of post-capitalist societies begins from Marx's assertion of the necessity of a phase of transition between capitalism and socialism (Birch, 1980). To move immediately after the global (no less than a merely national) overthrow of capitalism (an economy of generalized commodity production and growing inequalities within and between societies), to socialism, (an economy of democratic planning by the "freely associated producers" where social inequality and the state are "withering away") is impossible because capitalism prevents the even and steady development of labor productivity to its fullest potential. While the application of science and technology to the production process on a global scale in the late twentieth century would allow all humans' basic needs to be met relatively quickly and painlessly which would require restriction on elementary needs of people related to food, shelter, health and education (Blondel 1982).

In order for the entirety of humanity to enjoy a standard of living and, even more importantly, a reduced working day that will allow them to develop their fullest potential, eliminate economic inequalities and promote the "withering away" of the state, a further development of the global productive forces is necessary. This, in turn, requires the preservation of certain norms of "bourgeois distribution"—to each according to their labor, rather than their needs. The wage form, money, markets for certain consumer goods, and a state apparatus that ensures that all will work are necessary features of a society in transition to socialism. While the classical Marxist tradition believed that workers' democracy was possible and necessary to a successful transition, they also recognized that the maintenance of the state and "bourgeois norms of distribution" carried with it the possibility of the development of new forms of social inequality and conflict. However, revolutionary Marxists before the mid-1920s believed that a rapid victory of a world socialist revolution, especially its spread to the most industrially advanced capitalist societies, would greatly reduce these dangers (Breton and Ronald 1982).

The actual development of the world revolution in the twentieth century, the historic "stalemate in the international class struggle" that developed after 1923, confronted the revolutionary Marxist movement with a completely unexpected situation. Rather than beginning the global transition to socialism in a number of countries, including the more industrialized like Germany and Italy; the revolution was isolated in the most economically backward part of Europe, the former Russian empire. Russia's economic backwardness was compounded by the devastating effects of the civil war-the death of much of the generation of revolutionary workers who had made the October Revolution, extensive destruction of the country's meagre industrial base and the dispersal of the bulk of the industrial proletariat to the countryside. The failure of the German and Italian revolutions, for which the social-democratic bureaucracies bear major responsibility, created a situation in Russia where all of the inherent contradictions in a transitional society—between socialized production and bourgeois distribution—were intensified (Caiden and Siedentopp, 1982).

The absence of the two main preconditions for a successful transition to socialism—material abundance and a large and concentrated proletariat—created the environment for the growth of the Soviet bureaucracy. A layer of full-time state and party officials separate from the mass of workers emerged first to administer the distribution of scarce goods and services among the population. During the civil war, the number of state and party officials began to grow, as the Soviets requisitioned grain from the peasants to feed the urban workers and Red Army, and attempted to organize the shrinking state-owned industries for war production. The party and state bureaucracy mushroomed in the 1920s under the New Economic Policy, which allowed for the revival of commodity production and circulation in both the cities and countryside. In the late 1920s and 1930s, the Soviet bureaucracy deepened its grip over the state institutions and state owned means of production with the disastrous collectivization of agriculture and the creation of the "command economy." The bureaucracy, through its purge of the party and state apparatus in the late 1930s, dispersed and disorganized all opposition, particularly from the working class and peasantry, and consolidated their political power and enormous material privileges (Chowdhury, 1981).

Like Trotsky before him, Mandel emphasized the objective, material sources of the bureaucratization of the Soviet Union. On the one hand, the need for an agency, "above society", to distribute goods in a situation of extreme material scarcity provided a fertile environment for the growth of the party-state officialdom. On the other, the dispersal of the industrial proletariat through unemployment undermined the activist social base of Soviet democracy (Collins, 1980). However, both Mandel and Trotsky recognized that the Bolsheviks' made important subjective political errors that contributed to the victory of the Stalinist bureaucracy, particularly after the revolutionaries' victory in the civil war. Trotsky and Mandel argued that the decisions of the Tenth Congress of the Communist Party in 1921 — the blanket prohibition on all opposition parties from participation in the Soviets and the ban on opposition factions within the ruling party — "hindered rather than promoted the self-activity of the Russian workers" (Dogan 1975). These decisions undermined the ability of the Soviet workers, even the most politically active party members, from organizing themselves against the emerging bureaucracy, and gave these bureaucracies potent ideological weapons against any and all opposition within and without the ruling party. Trotsky recognized in 1937 the prohibition of factions which ended in a prohibition to think otherwise than the infallible leaders. The police-manufactured monolithism of the party resulted in a bureaucratic impunity which as become the source of all kinds of wantonness and corruption (Dudley, 1982).

In the last years of his life, Mandel forthrightly confronted the presence of unmistakably substitutionist elements in the politics of Lenin and Trotsky during the "dark years" of 1920-1921 (Etzioni 1983). While clearly embracing Marcel Liebman's characterization of pre-revolutionary Bolshevism as a stridently anti-substitutionist "libertarian Leninism," (Goodsell 1983) Mandel revealed how the Bolshevik leaders transformed violations of workers' democracy necessitated by the civil war into political virtues. Specifically, Lenin and Trotsky argued that temporary bans on opposition socialist parties, limitations of peasant and bourgeois suffrage, and empowering the Cheka to arrest, try and execute accused counter-revolutionaries without any political oversight were necessary and desirable features of proletarian rule. In numerous writings, both Lenin and Trotsky defended a clearly substitutionist conception of the relationship of the party and the working class. In Terrorism and Communism (which Mandel correctly declared "his worst book" (Hass 1979) and his polemics against the "Workers' Opposition", Trotsky proclaimed that the working class was a "wavering mass" incapable of exercising its rule directly and democratically. In the same years, Lenin repeatedly described the mass of workers as hopelessly divided, with sectors (the "labor aristocracy') corrupted by capital. In 1920-21, both proclaimed the party as the only force—even against the wishes and desires of the working class—capable of building socialism. Mandel did the revolutionary Marxist movement a great service by recognizing and rejecting this aspect of our tradition. As in the case of the labor bureaucracy in the capitalist countries, the ruling officialdoms in the former Soviet Union and the other bureaucratic societies developed their own, substitutionist world-view and political practice. The "dialectic of partial conquests" led the ruling bureaucracies in the east to embrace their particular version of "organizational fetishism"—the belief that the preservation of existing state-party institutions took priority over self-organization and self-activity of the working class. Internally, the Stalinist and neo-Stalinist bureaucrats' substitutionism privileged the "leading role of the party." The ruling Communist parties were the sole, legitimate representatives of the working class. They alone could defend the "historic interests" of the working class against all enemies, including "dissidents" and "deviationists" from within the ranks of the working class itself. The substitutionist ideology of the ruling bureaucracies provided ready made justifications for the brutal repression unleashed against the working class during the Soviet purges of the 1930s, the uprisings in East Germany, Poland and Hungary in the 1950s, against the "Prague Spring" in 1968, the mass strikes in Poland in 1971 and 1981, and the students and workers in Tiananmen Square in 1989. For the bureaucratic regimes, only the party, not the workers, was the ultimate guarantors of "true interests" of the proletariat. (Hawkee et al 1981)

Externally, the ruling bureaucracies' sought to subordinate the struggle of working people in other countries to the "defense of socialism in one (choose your favorite) country." Mandel extended Trotsky's analysis of the disastrous results of giving priority to the defense of some "socialist fatherland" abroad over the actual struggles of the workers and oppressed at home. The Communist parties in Germany in 1933, France and Spain in 1936-37, Greece after the second World War and in Indonesia in 1965 paid an extremely high price—massive repression and hundreds of thousands of militants murdered-for placing the diplomatic needs of the post—capitalist bureaucracies ahead of the needs of the class struggle in their own countries. Subservience to the ruling officialdoms in the east created the conditions for the gradual transformation the French, Italian and Spanish Communist parties into reformist parties; and led to the collapse of much of the revolutionary left of the 1960s that looked to the Maoist bureaucracy for political guidance (Heady, 1984).

Ultimately, the post-capitalist bureaucracies were incapable of consolidating a prosperous, attractive and stable alternative to capitalism. One of Mandel's major contributions has been his elaboration of Trotsky's insights into the limits of bureaucratic central planning: The progressive role of the Soviet bureaucracy coincides with the period devoted to introducing into the Soviet Union the most important elements of capitalist technique... It is possible to build gigantic factories according to a ready-made Western pattern by bureaucratic command-although, to be sure, at triple the normal cost. But the farther you go, the more the economy runs into the problem of quality, which slips out of the hands of a bureaucracy like a shadow... Under a nationalized economy, quality demands a democracy of producers and consumers, freedom of criticism and initiative-conditions incompatible with a totalitarian regime of fear, lies and flattery (Holley, 1983).

Mandel theoretically refined and empirically documented this thesis with extensive research (Hyndman, 1980). By substituting the party-state officialdom for the democratic decisions of workers and consumers, the Stalinized command economies were (and are in the case of China) left without any mechanism for insuring the long-term and continuous development of labor productivity. The post-capitalist bureaucracies were capable of organizing extensive growth, forcing millions of uprooted peasants to labor in plants that reproduced the labor processes of the capitalist west, producing an "one time only" increase in labor productivity. However, they floundered when faced with organizing intensive growth, the continuous replacement of labor with new technologies and production of new items of consumption. The bureaucracy lacked either the "whip of competition" that ensures that each capitalist firm continuously reduces necessary labor through mechanization, or the democratic control over economic decisions by the "freely associated producers and consumers" with an interest in reducing their labor time and insuring quality items of individual and collective consumption (Hyndman 1980). As a result, the bureaucratic economies were under no economic or political compulsion to develop new technique or economize on the use of resources. The result was that "a general lack of responsibility, and indifference to the factory's performance is therefore a characteristic feature of the system and threatens the USSR with stagnation and decline." (Johnson, 1973) The fate of the bureaucratic command economies in Eastern Europe and the ex-USSR tragically confirmed Mandel and Trotsky's theses.

Unlike Trotsky, who confined himself to a general call for the restoration of soviet democracy through an anti-bureaucratic workers' revolution, Mandel presented a detailed model of democratic centralist economic planning. A global "self-administered" economy would be founded upon democratic councils of producers and consumers. The officials of these councils would be elected by the entire adult population, would be subject to immediate recall and would be paid the average salary of a skilled worker. These democratic institutions of workers' power, created through anti-capitalist revolutions in the west and anti-bureaucratic revolutions in the east, would be articulated at the international, national, industrial and office, factory or neighborhood level, where:

> Decisions should be taken at the level at which they can most easily be implemented. And they should be taken at the level where the greatest percentage of people actually affected by them can be involved in the decision-making process (Khan, 1980). Put simply, international and national bodies would be empowered to draw up the basic outlines of the economic plan, while industrial, regional or plant-office bodies would decide how to implement their particular parts of the plan in consultation with those who will consume their product (Kornaghan, 1982). In order for democratic "self-administration" to be effective, the working class must be able to express their needs and desires in the planning process and there must be mechanisms for the correction of social and economic miscalculations. According to Mandel, political pluralism is required to allow the working class, in all its heterogeneity, to effectively control the planning process. Without the right of all political currents (including ideologically pro-capitalist tendencies) to organize political parties, have access (in proportion to their numbers) to the media and to organize demonstrations and other non-violent actions to advance their particular view point, central planning will not be able to utilize productive resources efficiently and raise the productivity of labor. Mandel also recognized that formally democratic institutions and the rigorous guarantee of political rights for all sectors of the population, while necessary conditions for democratic socialist rule, are not sufficient. There are also crucial social and economic conditions, most

importantly the radical reduction of working time for the mass of the population so that all "have the time to administer the affairs of their workplace or neighborhood" (Lee et al, 1970). Such a reduction of the working day would allow most of humanity to spend 3-4 hours a day in the production of goods or provision of services and another 3-4 hours a day in the work of social self-administration. In order to abolish the division between mental and manual labor, the basis of bureaucracy, there must be generalized access to education, culture and literacy, which assumes a high level of material abundance and labor productivity. This, Mandel asserted, will only be possible when not only bureaucratic rule has been replaced in the east, but capitalism has been overthrown in a number of advanced industrial societies and their vast productive potential freed (Mathur, 1983).

Mandel, like Marx and Trotsky before him, recognized that commodity production and circulation, the market, would survive for a considerable period after the overthrow of capitalism on a world scale. Mandel agreed with Alec Nove, the most sophisticated theorist of "market socialism" that "the radical suppression of residual market relations" in any of the post-capitalist societies was not "presently desirable or practical." In fact, Mandel saw elements of Nove's model of "feasible socialism" as similar to his own conception of the combination of market and plan in a democratically ruled society in transition to socialism (Medina, 1982). Mandel's disagreement with the "market socialists" was their claim that commodity production was a permanent and unalterable feature of economic life. For Nove, the complexity of economic decisions in an industrialized economy and the "unlimited wants" of human beings made the abolition of scarcity, the foundation of commodity production, impossible. The withering away of the market was possible for two reasons according to Mandel. First, a system of "articulated self-management" could allocate most of the thousands of decisions necessary to a planned economy to different democratically organized bodies, overcoming the problem of "too many decisions." Second, it was possible to envision a "saturation of demand" for goods and services once basic material needs was satisfied. Mandel rejected the simplistic notion of "human nature' that underlies both neo-classical economics and the theories of "market socialism":

> The continual accumulation of more and more goods... is by no means a universal or even predominant feature of human behavior. The development of talents and inclinations for their own sake; the protection of health and life; care for children; the development of rich social relations as a prerequisite of mental stability and happiness-all these become major motivations once basic material needs have been satisfied. One has only to look at how the upper reaches of the bourgeoisie conduct themselves with regard to food, clothing, housing, furniture or 'cultural goods' to note that for those who already 'live under communism', rational consumption takes the place of a restless pursuit of more (Murray, 1978). Mandel, responding to the rise of the environmental movements of the last twenty five years, incorporated a detailed discussion of the relationship of different forms of social and economic organization to the natural environment. Mandel addressed two objections to the Marxian vision of socialism raised in the "Green" analysis of the rape of the environment in both capitalist and bureaucratic economies. Various "Green" theorists argue that the Marxian vision of a future society based upon the abolition of material scarcity would place an unbearable strain on the physical resources of the planet and lead to an ecological. disaster. Mandel pointed to the scale of socially wasted resources under both capitalism and the bureaucratic command economies. The immediate abolition of the arms industry alone would free up tremendous resources for socially useful production (based upon renewable energy sources, environmentally safe technologies, etc.) that could provide an adequate

standard of living for the bulk of the worlds' population without thrusting new demands upon the finite capacities of the planet. As the basic, material needs for physical security and gratification (food, clothing, shelter, medical care, education) are met, priority could be given to meeting the non-material needs for "self-actualization" (cultural, political, intellectual and personal development), needs whose satisfaction do not require utilizing finite natural resources.

The second "Green" critique of Marxism, based upon the experience of ecological disaster in the former USSR and Eastern Europe, claims that centrally planned economies are no more ecologically friendly than market-capitalist economies. For Mandel, the destruction of the environment in the east flowed from the same bureaucratic mismanagement that gave rise to systematic waste of labor power and other resources. In other words, the absence of any democratic accountability on the parts of central planners and industrial managers allowed them to systematically befoul the physical environment in the east. By contrast, a democratically planned economy has the potential to avoid the ecological disasters that characterize both capitalism and the bureaucratic command economies. Workers and consumers actively involved in formulating and implementing an economic plan have a com pelling interest in developing labor processes that will neither destroy the health of those directly involved in production, nor befoul the air and water that all must breath and drink. In addition, the possibility of democratic "self-correction" would minimize environmental damage that might ensue from workers' attempting to raise their standard of living without consideration of its effects on future generations (Nachmias, 1980).

Mandel's elaboration and extension of Trotsky's theory of the post-capitalist bureaucracies not only provides an powerful alternative to liberal, social-democratic and Stalinist theories of bureaucracy, but to other Marxian theories as well. In particular, Mandel has produced an extensive critique of the theory that the former USSR, Eastern Europe and

China were "state capitalist" social formations. The notion that economies where the main means of production are allocated according to conscious planning decisions, however bureaucratically mismanaged, and not according to differential profit rates and prices of production; where labor-power is no longer a commodity and a state monopoly of foreign trade mediates the effects of global capitalist competition on the planned economy are capitalist is theoretically and empirically untenable. This theory, as Mandel pointed out numerous times, does violence both to the Marxian theory of capitalist accumulation and the empirical reality of the bureaucratic economies. Mandel's critique of the other major alternative Marxian theory of the bureaucratic regimes, the theory of "bureaucratic collectivism", is not as rigorous as his dissection of the theory of "state-capitalism." For Mandel, like Trotsky, the bureaucracy in the post-capitalist societies is a caste, a social layer that, unlike a social class, plays no necessary role in social production. The 'parasitic' relationship between the bureaucracy and the planned economy deprives these post-capitalist societies of the social coherence of an established mode of production. Since the late 1930s, various Marxist critics of Stalinism have challenged this theory, arguing that the bureaucracy was a new exploiting class that organized a new, post-capitalist mode of production in the ex-USSR and the eastern bloc countries (Owusu, 1978). The theory of "bureaucratic collectivism" has been held by a wide variety of revolutionary socialists, including many prominent anti-bureaucratic activists in the former eastern bloc (Peagels, 1984). Its theoretical attraction is not surprising. On the one hand, it avoids the problems of the theory of "state capitalism". On the other it avoids the complexities and ambiguities of Mandel and Trotsky's theory of a 'transitional society' by situating the bureaucracy and the command economy in the familiar Marxian categories of class and mode of production.

Mandel offers two different criticisms of the theory of bureaucratic collectivism. The first and, in our opinion, the weaker response points to the survival of commodity production and circulation in the bureaucratic economies. The survival of the wage form, the impact of the world market, etc. are features of any transitional society, and run counter to the logic of planning. The hybrid combination of an allocative and a commodity-producing economy, in which the law of value operates but does not hold sway. And this influence of the law of value ultimately sets immovable limits to bureaucratic despotism. This is what theorists of 'bureaucratic collectivism'...fail to see... For a 'new', 'bureaucratic' non-capitalist mode of production to emerge, the Soviet bureaucracy would have to have liberated itself once and for all from the influence of the law of value (Handbook of Information on the Philippine civil service. 1984).

This line of argument is open to several important criticisms. First, Mandel and Trotsky's notion that the bureaucracy's privileges and power are derived primarily from the survival of "bourgeois norms of distribution" is problematic. Much of the bureaucracy's substantially higher standard of living compared to the working class was not derived from their superior incomes and market access to commodities. It was instead based upon their political power, derived from their command of the state apparatus and the state owned means of production, to gain preferential non-market, non-commodity access to consumer goods through special stores and "jumping the queue" for relatively scarce consumer goods like cars, housing, etc.

Second, and more importantly, there have been numerous societies where non-capitalist modes of production coexisted with quite extensive commodity circulation and where "the privileges of the privileges of the dominant classes... are mainly confined to the realm of private consumption, [and] they have no long-term interest in a sustained increase in productivity" (Poudyal, 1984). European feudalism, slavery in both classical antiquity and the so-called "new world", and the various "Asiatic" societies all allowed for, and in some cases promoted extensive commodity production, although not the generalized commodity production possible only under capitalism. These same modes of production were dominated by exploiting classes whose privilege were confined to private consumption, and who were unable to organize the labor process of their direct producers in a manner that allowed for sustained increases in productivity. In fact, it is only under capitalism that the ruling class' privileges extend to real possession of the means of production-the ability to organize the labor process. Thus, the bourgeoisie is the first ruling class in world history to be both capable of, and compelled to continually raise the productivity of labor through mechanization (Price, 1975).

The introduction of "market mechanisms" into the bureaucratic command economies during the past twenty-five years has demonstrated the possibility of combining "market" and "plan" without undermining bureaucratic privilege and power. The ruling officialdom in Yugoslavia, Poland, Hungary, China and the former USSR all introduced "market reforms" at different points in the last forty years in attempts to overcome the chronic stagnation of labor productivity in the eastern bloc. As we know, these reforms were singularly ineffective in either stimulating intensive economic development or lessening bureaucratic despotism. If anything, market mechanisms enriched the bureaucracy and sharpened its antagonism with the working class and peasantry without forcing productive units to introduce new labor processes or use materials more efficiently (Quah, 1978). In sum, while the combination of planning and commodity production is a necessary feature of every society in transition from capitalism to socialism, the combination of plan and market is not a sufficient basis for rejecting the notion that a new mode of production developed in the former USSR, eastern Europe and China.

Mandel's second, and stronger critique of the bureaucracy as a "new ruling class" points to the profound contradiction between bureaucratic power and the logic of effective economic planning (Robin, 1984) First, the bureaucracy has a "parasitic" relationship to economic planning-it is theoretically unnecessary to a planned economy. The working class could quite as easily organize a planned economy without a privileged layer of officials, although, at least initially, not without specialists and technicians. By comparison, one cannot conceive of an economy of generalized commodity production without capitalists and workers.

Second, the bureaucracy's attempt to enrich itself undermines the effectivity of the planning process. At every level of the command economy, bureaucrats systematically hide resources, whether labor power, raw material or machinery, in order to meet production targets and obtain bonuses in the forms of cash or access to better housing, vacations and the like. Bureaucratic secrecy makes effective economic planning impossible. Without realistic information about resources and productive capacity it is impossible to set realistic production targets. By contrast, the bourgeoisie's efforts to enrich itself deepens the conditions of capitalist competition as each capitalist attempts to undercut all others and increase their market share by lowering costs. The individual self-interest of the capitalist coincides with the operation of the law of value, but the individual self-interest of the bureaucrat runs counter to the logic of economic planning.

Finally, the contradictions between the privileges of the bureaucracy and the logic of planning deprives the bureaucratic economies of any internally generated dynamic of crisis and recovery. While the bureaucracy's privilege undermines the effectivity of planning, leading to declining rates of growth in the 1970s and 1980s, there was no mechanism internal to the bureaucratic economy that could resolve the crisis. Only a profound shift in the relationship of social forces politically, either a workers' anti-bureaucratic revolution or capitalist restoration, could establish the conditions for renewed growth. Capitalism's inherent drive to replace human labor generates declining profit rates and periodic "long-waves" of economic crisis. However, capitalism generates its own solution to these prolonged crises. The massive destruction of inefficient capitals and "redundant" labor during an economic collapse restores the conditions of profitable accumulation and sparks a new "long-wave" of expansion (Raksasatya et al, 1980). Thus, there are no "terminal crises" of capitalism. The rule of capital, like the feudal aristocracy and other ruling classes rooted in modes of production, must be overthrown. The strongest historical validation of Trotsky and Mandel's thesis that the former USSR and eastern European regimes were not rooted in a new mode of production was the rapidity with which they collapsed in 1989-1991. Bureaucratic rule in these societies was not overthrown by either the working class or imperialism, but imploded as a result of chronic economic stagnation. Not surprisingly, the social formations that emerged in eastern Europe and the former Soviet Union have yet to make a successful transition to capitalism.

While Mandel and Trotsky's theory of the "transitional" character of the post-capitalist societies remains convincing, their claim that these regimes were "bureaucratized" forms of the proletarian dictatorship is open to question. Through the early years of the Russian revolution, revolutionary Marxists generally equated the workers' state with highly democratic forms of popular participation and power, in particular with the Paris Commune of 1871 and the workers', soldiers and peasants councils that had arisen in Russia, Germany, Hungary and Italy between 1917 and 1921. The defeat of the central and western European revolutions and the devastation of the civil war undermined the viability of the Russian Soviets as organs of popular power. For Lenin and Trotsky, the working class character of the Russian state was preserved in the Community party, which organized the most active and radical workers. However, the "rule of the party" proved an inadequate basis for preserving even an indirect form of workers' self-government. The decline of party democracy after the 1921 ban on factions and the consolidation of the party-state bureaucracy in the late 1920s transformed the Soviet Communist party into the political instrument of the Stalinist officialdom.

By the late 1930s, Trotsky argued that the Soviet Union remained a workers' state, despite the "political expropriation" of the working class, because the bureaucracy continued to defend the social and economic "conquests of the October Revolution" - nationalized property, central planning and a state monopoly on foreign trade. The Soviet regime was a form of "bonapartism", similar to both feudal Absolutism, where the aristocracy ceded power to a royal bureaucracy that preserved feudalism, and fascism, where the bourgeoisie ceded power to a petty-bourgeoisie that safeguarded the conditions of capitalist accumulation. Thus, the mainstream of the Trotskyist movement, including Mandel, saw the USSR, and later eastern Europe, China and Vietnam, as "bureaucratized workers' states" where the working class ruled but did not govern (Sghaffer, 1974).

There are compelling theoretical reasons for maintaining the theory of the "bureaucratized workers' states." Most importantly, the traditional Trotskyist conception is consistent with the fundamental Marxian axiom that every society torn by social conflicts, no matter how unstable and transitional, are ruled by a single social class. As Perry Anderson argued, Trotsky's interpretation of Stalinism:

> ...provides a theory of the phenomenon of Stalinism in a long historical temporality, congruent with the fundamental categories of classical Marxism. At every point in his account of the nature of the Soviet bureaucracy, Trotsky sought to situate it in the logic of successive modes of production and transitions between them, with corresponding class powers and political regimes, that he inherited from Marx, Engels or Lenin.... Because he could think of the emergence and consolidation of Stalinism in a historical time-span of this epochal character, he avoided the explanations of hasty journalism and improvised confections of new classes or modes of production, unanchored in historical materialism, which marked the reaction of many of his contemporaries (Gole et al, 1984).

These strengths, however, conceal profound problems with the concept of a "workers' state" where the workers rule, but do not govern. The analogy with feudal absolutism and capitalist dictatorships tends to obscure the differentia specifica of the transition to socialism. First, neither the feudal nor capitalist modes of production emerged from the struggles of classes self-consciously attempting to create new forms of society. Instead, feudalism and capitalism arose out of the struggles of already propertied classes to consolidate and extend their class domination. Socialism, by contrast, is the first form of society created in a conscious struggle by a propertyless social class, the working class. Further, both feudalism and capitalism are reproduced through a "blind economic logic" that operates "behind the back" of both the economically dominant classes and the direct producers. The feudal aristocracy and the bourgeoisie can remain socially dominant without directly dominating the state. Socialism is the first form of society based on conscious and deliberate planning of economic development. These profound differences between socialism and all previous forms of social labor led Mandel to argue in his last major work:

> There is no way in which the working class can rule without governing. It has to exercise power simultaneously within enterprise and branch, municipality and region, as well as at the aggregate levels of the state and the national economy; if it is to 'rule' in any real and direct sense of the word: to take the key decisions about economic, social, and cultural priorities in the allocation of scarce resources. Thus, the functional division of the proletariat, between those who 'professionally exercise power' and the mass of the class, sets in motion a social process which suppresses the direct collective rule of the class as such (Gans et al, 1986).

Here Mandel provided compelling reasons for rejecting the analogy between absolutism, fascism and bureaucratic rule that he and Trotsky upon which they had based their notion of a "bureaucratized workers' state."

In other writings, Mandel attempted to defend the "bureaucratized workers' state" theory by arguing that the Stalinist bureaucracy was a privileged layer of the working class which had usurped power from the rest of the class. First, he claimed that the bureaucracy's derived most of its privileges in the form of wages:

> ...the bureaucracy, since it does not own the means of production, participates in distribution of the national income exclusively as a function of remuneration for its labor-power. This entails many

privileges, but it is a form of remuneration that does not differ qualitatively from remuneration in the form of a salary (Petiteville, 1998).

This claim is open to two criticisms. First, as we have already seen, the bureaucracy secures much of its greater levels of consumption through non-wage, non-market access to consumer goods. The officialdom's access to special stores, dachas and the like derives from their political power - their domination of the state apparatus and control over state owned means of production. Second, the wage form, while a necessary characteristic of the working class is not sufficient to define a social group as part of the proletariat. In the capitalist social formations, top and middle level corporate executives receive salaries. Even when these executives do not own stock (although most do), they are part of the capitalist class because they command the labor-power of others and dispose of the means of production. Similarly, it can be argued that a much larger layer of wage-earners-low level supervisors, technicians and professionals-are not part of the working class in advanced capitalism. Many contemporary Marxists view these groups as forming a new middle class, produced by of the concentration and centralization of capital and the systematic application of science to production under capitalism. Mandel also argued that the post-capitalist bureaucracy was a layer of the working class because of the ease by which individual workers moved into the bureaucracy.For it is absolutely certain that a good number of today's bureaucrats, in this broad and real sense of the term, are not merely the sons and daughters of workers but even former workers themselves... The particular structure of society in the Soviet Union enables the bureaucracy to absorb the sons and daughters of workers, and even workers themselves, into the apparatus. Not into the summits of the apparatus, but into positions much higher than those of the so-called middle classes in the advanced capitalist countries. Granting much higher, but clearly slowing, rates of upward social mobility between the working class and the bureaucracy in the east than between the working and capitalist classes in the west, this argument remains theoretically unconvincing.

From a Marxian perspective, classes are defined by their objective relationship to social production, not the social origins of their members. Put simply, contemporary capitalist societies could experience a significant increase in social mobility-the wholesale proletarianization of the bourgeoisie and the bourgeoisification of a small minority of the working class-without altering the structural relationship between capital and wage labor. The fact that many, or even most, post-capitalist bureaucrats came from the working class did not make the officialdom part of the proletariat.

Our discussion of the post-capitalist bureaucracy leaves us in a difficult theoretical position. On the one hand, there is little theoretical or empirical basis for the notion that the bureaucracy is a new social class based in a new mode of production. The post-capitalist command economies were transitional societies, whose progress toward socialism was blocked by the rule of an officialdom whose power and privileges made effective economic planning impossible. On the other hand, it is extremely difficult to argue that the bureaucratic regimes were "deformed" forms of the proletarian dictatorship. The working class in the east neither ruled nor governed, and the bureaucracy was not a "layer" of the working class. This leaves us unable to identify what class ruled the former USSR, Eastern Europe and China. At best, we can say that these societies were "historical abortions", the product of the "global stalemate of the class struggle" in the twentieth century. They were highly unstable, transitional societies governed by bureaucracies, who excluded the working classes from any real or formal social and political power, but were not themselves ruling classes. Their rapid implosion in 1989-1991 demonstrated their profound instability and the bureaucracy's thoroughly "parasitic" character. This is the best understanding we as Marxists can have of these societies based upon our experience of their actual historical evolution. Further theoretical clarification would require the emergence of new bureaucratized transitional societies, which would provide us with additional "raw material" for our theory. For that reason, we have reason to hope this is a theoretical issue that will never be settled decisively.

## Bureaucracy in England and USA

By the end of the eighteenth century systematic concern with the theory and practice of regularized administration as a central function of government was burgeoning throughout Europe. Growth in population, production and trade, the conversion of wars from dynastic into national wars, the acquisition of colonies, the foundation and expansion of great capital cities, all played a role. So did the increasing social importance of the literate middle classes and the decline of an aristocracy deriving its claim to authority from origin and military conquests. Above all, however, the Enlightenment, and its heirs in England, the philosophical radicals, were introducing, or strengthening, demands that governments perform, that they improve the position of their people and the public welfare, that they convert royal servants into public servants, the crown into the state, office into a public trust. The Industrial Revolution and the growth of scientific knowledge intensified these developments and added yet other dimensions. These were a much more advanced division of labour, increasing need and respect for specialization and technical knowledge (both in the broad and in the narrow sense of 'technical') and a much more urgent sense of economic development, public health and human progress, to which government and administration might and should make a significant contribution. As the nineteenth century progressed, the accelerated building of public roads and facilities, the introduction of gas, electricity and the telephone all required corps of officials with a degree of training. So did the introduction of military conscription and of new scientific and technological services for modern armies, and then navies. The industrial technology itself and later a host of scientific technologies, having extended enormously the harm that human actions and possessions might do to others, provoked—partly through outrage over individual mishaps or abuses more and more government action, inspection and control. All this encouraged governments to perform new functions and made possible and necessary the employment of many more civil servants on the basis of ever-increasing revenue through taxation.

Even in the eighteenth century, theorists of 'police' (the polity) and of political economy had emphasized the role of centrally made and directed laws, capable of clarification, improvement and organization into a coherent body of rational law. Karl Marx in his 'Eighteen Brumaire' and Friedrich Engels in his 'Introduction to Marx's Civil War in France' characterize USA and England as two rare exceptions in Bourgeois society viewing the matter in retrospective, it becomes fairly obvious that Bureaucracy in large measure has remained an institution alien to those two countries until, at least the turning point of the third quarter of the Nineteenth century. This apparent time lag in the emergence of bureaucracy can be explained with reference to the original function (i.e. removal of all feudal hindrances to bourgeois development) and dual nature (i.e. anti feudal and anti proletarianism) of the organs of centralized bourgeois state power (Kurthan, 1970). Four decades after the passing remarks of Marx and Engels, on the subject of Bureaucracy in England, Lenin wrote "Today in 1917 in the epoch of the first great imperialist war this distinction of Marx becomes unusual and England and America, the greatest and last representatives of Anglo Saxon liberty in the sense of the absence of militarism and bureaucracy, have today completely rolled down into the dirty, bloody morass of military bureau critic institutions common to all Europe, subordinating all else to themselves, crushing all else under themselves". He further noted The USA and England were the two meccas of Bureaucracy. Subsequent writers on bureaucracy and the Enlightenment have reminded us of striking contemporary quotations: A properly constituted state must be exactly analogous to a machine, in which all the wheels and gears are precisely adjusted to one another; and the ruler must be the foreman, the mainspring, or the soul—if one may use the expression—which sets everything in motion. [JHG von Justi, 1761]. In eighteenth-century France, as a modern scholar has put it: the word 'machine' has been increasingly used to describe administrative organizations. By the end of the eighteenth century the machine had become an obsessive image. Anson used it to describe the projected Ministry of the Interior, Camus to describe the entire administration, Marat to represent municipal administrations, and to sum up, the machine image in the writings of Lebrun, Roederer, Laffon de Ladebat and many others seems to show that this generation thought of administrative and political agencies as analogous to machines. The other possible analogy, comparing the organization to the human body as Hobbes for instance had done, seldom appears in the writings of the late eighteenth-century French reformers and revolutionaries. [J F Bosher, 1970]. The French Revolution stood for the consummation of the Enlightenment. It saw government and administration as needing to be based on principles of rationality, welfare and utility. But it also saw government and its officials as servants of the people. It rejected, at least in principle, the notion that the fonctionnaire was part of a caste or class having a special standing in society by virtue of 'being an office-holder. In principle, bureaucrats were being robbed of their special standing as part of a ranked society or as an extension of royal power and prestige. The bureaucracy was being transformed into a civil service. For much of the nineteenth century, the new capitalist order was seen as incorporating the reality of the demand for parliamentary democracy, legal equality for citizens, the guarantee of (individual) human rights, primarily against the state, and a defeasible (i.e. contestable) presumption against interference by the community or its actual or self-proclaimed representatives. Basically, however, capitalism was an economic concept. It was the society of free enterprise, of industrial production for a market on the basis of private ownership, freedom of contract and freedom from unnecessary state controls or gratuitous government planning. Its supporters held, as an article of faith, that individual effort and commercial enterprise were the mainsprings of progress, the source of vigour and inventiveness, the creators of wealth. Governments and their servants were essentially parasitic. Where eighteenth- and even early nineteenth-century attacks on bureaucracy emphasized its nature as a caste, its pseudo-aristocratic arrogance, its readiness to dominate, the attack shifts—as the century progresses—to the view that the power of the state is or will be at the expense of the development of citizens, of communal institutions and of individual enterprise.

John Stuart Mill, in his Principles of Political Economy, opposed 'concentrating in a dominant bureaucracy all the skill and experience in the management of large interests, and the power of organized action, existing in the community'. In Representative Government, he concluded that 'the comparison ... as to the intellectual attributes of a government, has to be made between a representative democracy and a bureaucracy; all other governments may be left out of the account'. Bureaucrats are expert; they operate by well-tried and well-considered maxims and are staffed by trained people. Nevertheless, 'The disease which afflicts bureaucratic governments, and which they usually die of, is routine. They perish by the immutability of their maxims; and, still more, by the universal law that whatever becomes a routine loses its vital principle ...'. On Liberty, Mill had gone still further. Expanding functions of government and the greater efficiency of government would end in monopolizing the talent of the nation — the bureaucracy would do everything and nothing could be done outside it or against its wishes. For Bagehot, the skills of a bureaucracy had only the appearance of science; they were in truth inconsistent with the proper principles of the art of business. Herbert Spencer, inexplicably but nevertheless most effectively the general and political mentor of a generation, attacked the Liberals in 1884 for espousing state intervention: 'Increasing power of a growing administrative organization is accompanied by decreasing power of the rest of society to resist its further growth and control bureaucracy. The multiplicity of careers opened by a developing bureaucracy tempts members of society to acquiesce in or favour such further growth.' F.C. Montague, in *The Limits of Individual Liberty* (1884), developed the same theme, distinguishing the regulated servitude in which the citizens of continental bureaucracies lived from the identification between administration and the community assured in England by Parliament, the law courts and municipal liberties. For Ramsay Muir, writing on 'Bureaucracy in England' in 1910, the persistent and powerful influence of great permanent officials in the government of England constituted a pernicious and essentially un-English bureaucratization of British government. The paradox of capitalism lay in its principled opposition to bureaucratic management being accompanied by a process of economic development and rationalization which sought state support where it was advantageous and which led both to the bureaucratization of capitalist enterprises as they grew in size and scope and to the extension of the ideology of rational planning and calculation in social life. For Weber, bureaucrats were becoming as inescapable in business as in government. For Joseph Schumpeter, the 'trustified' firm lost the entrepreneurial spirit of capitalism and became a planned and bureaucratized institution; for many a subsequent writer, the internal economic organization and problems of General Motors and the USSR have had remarkable similarities.

Only during late 1930s, some thinkers, mostly ex-Marxists, began to see bureaucracies in modern societies, or in modern societies of a certain sort, as new ruling classes. A new form of society—bureaucratic collectivism—was successfully taking over by assaulting and appropriating capitalist power and property. This had happened in the Soviet Union and—though only partly—in Nazi Germany, Fascist Italy and militarist Japan. Under bureaucratic collectivism, the ruling bureaucracy formed a class which collectively exploited the mass of the population and drew surplus value from its work. Rizzi himself believed that bureaucratic collectivism was historically progressive, a transitional social formation between capitalism and socialism. In Lucien Laurat's Marxism and Democracy (London, 1940, a translation from the French original, Paris, London, 1939) and James Burnham's The Managerial Revolution (London, 1941), matters were taken further. Laurat pointed to the growing power of a new class—pluto-technocratic in the west and bureau-technocratic in the USSR; Burnham noted that the modern corporation was increasingly run by managers and not by its owners (who were often fragmented: trust companies, pension funds, small and large individual shareholders etc.). He saw such managers as introducing managerial societies throughout the world. For all these writers, working out of the Marxist heritage, it was important to show that the new ruling bureaucracies were in fact owners of the means of production, through their individual or collective control, even if they were not legal owners.

'Bureaucracy' was arguably the most important concept to shape the organisation of the public sector in the UK and many other parts of the world during the 20th century. During this period, the root causes of many socio economic problems were regarded by successive governments on both the left and right of the political spectrum as being organisational or institutional in nature. As such, organisational change was presented as an important part of the solution to a whole range of problems, including poverty, unemployment, housing, health, education, sanitation and water supply. That is not to say that efforts had not been made previously to address some of these problems, but bureaucracy was regarded by its advocates as a far superior organisational model which offered greater efficiency and reliability. Drawing on the definition proposed by the organisational and social theorist Max Weber, Beetham (1996) identified four main features of bureaucracy. First, bureaucracy is characterised by hierarchy in which each official or organisational unit has a clearly defined competence and is answerable to a superior for its performance. Second, bureaucracy offers continuity within established career structures and rule governed procedures. Third, bureaucracy operates according to impersonality so that work is conducted without arbitrariness or favouritism by adhering to established rules. Finally, bureaucracy is defined by expertise among officials who are selected according to merit, trained to perform their functions and positioned to control access to privileged knowledge. The early advocates of the bureaucratic approach regarded these four features as highly desirable and also attainable qualities which could be applied prescriptively to improve organisational performance. However, critics have argued that bureaucracy has fallen below expectations when put into practice. Others have pointed towards the tendency for bureaucracies to become overly protective of their own organisational territories and areas of competence, while at the same time exhibiting a capacity to continually expand into new policy arenas. Problems thus defined as institutional and societal rather than moral and individual cried out for collective, professional solutions rather than moral discipline and exhortation. And once the legislative and administrative treatment began, the process of professionalisation and feedback set it, by which the welfare professionals uncovered new problems which demanded further legislative and administrative solutions.... As such, it was not only the establishment of government bureaucracies that defined much of public policy in the last century but also the idea that professional and bureaucratic responses rather than political, personal, or cooperative solutions were necessary to deal with major societal problems. Furthermore, their professional status enabled bureaucrats to exert influence on political decision making while at the same time avoiding the need for public scrutiny and debate because of their exclusive claims on knowledge and expertise. A further criticism of bureaucracy concerns the lack of attention given to the external environment of both public and private organisations. Industrial economies and the effects of globalisation started to be felt. Trist (1983) labelled this new type of environment as a 'turbulent field'. Bureaucracy was designed for functional pecialisation whereas many present day societal problems are framed in ways that transcend the conventional categories of economy, society and environment. The concept of sustainable development is particularly important in this regard. While many governments have adopted sustainability as a fundamental development principle and goal, they continue to rely on bureaucratic structures and processes for policy delivery. A popular argument in academic fields such as planning, governance and inter organisational relations is that the increasing complexity, uncertainty and change in the environment of the last couple of decades have resulted in a period of institutional adaptation involving a shrinking of bureaucracy and the emergence of new styles of governance. Indeed, the term 'governance' is often used symbolically to refer to a new policy centric regime involving complex networks of public and private actors engaged in collaborative policy making through open processes of dialogue, social learning and negotiation. Evidence of the emergence of these sorts of complex arrangements in a variety of different public policy arenas has fuelled a debate about the role of bureaucracy in modern society. According to Laffin (1998), two distinct schools of thought can be identified within the debate. Within the 'neo bureaucratic' school, recent institutional reforms are seen as the product of politicians and policy makers who are imposing 'new public management' principles and practices across different policy arenas to improve efficiency and effectiveness. The resulting complex systems of committees, advisory boards, round tables and working parties etc. are assigned specific roles and responsibilities that are, nonetheless, authorised and controlled by bureaucratic masters to varying degrees. In contrast, the 'post bureaucratic' school argues that a much more fundamental shift is underway that involves self organising inter organisational policy networks, which function collaboratively and with only very limited input or influence from formal government. According to this view, the organisation of public policy is becoming far more diverse, with private or non profit organisations taking on policy making and implementation roles previously performed by local authorities or other public bodies. In this sort of governance arrangement, relationships between policy makers and service providers are more likely to be based on negotiation as equal partners, or quasi market arrangements, rather than on conventional hierarchical control arrangements. Consequently, it is argued that the previously clearly defined vertical and lateral boundaries among elected politicians, appointed officials, public agencies and private or voluntary organisations have blurred with the diffusion of power within society.

## Conclusion

Mandel, working from the foundation provided by Luxemburg and Trotsky, has provided us with the most theoretically rigorous and empirically well-founded Marxian discussion of bureaucracy to date. Mandel's analysis of the labor officialdom under capitalism and the ruling bureaucracy in the post-capitalist social formations is a powerful alternative to the liberal, social-democratic and Stalinist theories that claim that the rule of a full-time corps of non-propertied officials is an unavoidable feature of modern society. Rather than an unavoidable development in human history, bureaucracy is the product of specific and historically transitory social relations and material forces of production. Mandel does much more than demonstrate that democratic self-organization of the working class in both capitalist and post-capitalist societies are possible. His theory of bureaucracy, together with his investigations into the dynamics of capitalist accumulation in the twentieth century, points to the necessity of working class self-emancipation as the only basis for human liberation and survival. The notions that the labor bureaucrats can defend the gains of workers under capitalism or that the ruling bureaucracies can construct a viable alternative to capitalism has proven to be thoroughly utopian. The material position and self-interest of the reformist bureaucracies in the west have led them to disorganize and demobilize the working class and surrender, practically without a struggle, most of the hard fought for gains of the past half century. The material position and self-interest of the ruling bureaucracies in the east have led them to undermine the planning process and waste precious human and natural resources. In short, the failure of bureaucratic strategies for gradually reforming capitalism or building an authoritarian alternative to it have necessarily floundered on the social position of the bureaucracies in both the capitalist and post-capitalist social formations. Mandel's theory of bureaucracy is one of the central scientific foundations of our revolutionary socialist political project in the late twentieth century. Not goodwill, democratic idealism or a commitment to an egalitarian morality alone, but a scientific understanding of the role of the officialdom of the workers' movement and post-capitalist societies leads us to defend working class self-emancipation as the only practical alternative to capitalist barbarism. The theory of the firm has many applications to political markets, and principal-agent theory in particular has been used to describe the relationship between Congress and the bureaucracy. The principal-agent model of the bureaucracy addresses the importance of property rights and contracts in political markets. In this regard, the development of this model parallels the evolution of the theory of the firm that has stressed the significance of transactions costs associated with using the price mechanism. (Friedrich Engels: *The Origin of the Family, Private Property and the State*). A properly constituted state must be exactly analogous to a machine, in which all the wheels and gears are precisely adjusted to one another; and the ruler must be the foreman, the mainspring, or the soul — if one may use the expression— which sets everything in motion, recent institutional reforms are seen as the product of politicians and policy makers who are imposing 'new public management' principles and practices across different policy arenas to improve efficiency and effectiveness. The resulting complex systems of committees, advisory boards, round tables and working parties etc. are assigned specific roles and responsibilities that are, nonetheless, authorised and controlled by bureaucratic masters to varying degrees. In contrast, the 'post bureaucratic' school argues that a much more fundamental shift is underway that involves self organising inter organisational policy networks, which function collaboratively and with only very limited input or influence from formal government. According to this view, the organisation of public policy is becoming far more diverse, with private or non profit organisations taking on policy making and implementation roles previously performed by local authorities or other public bodies. In this sort of governance arrangement, relationships between policy makers and service providers are more likely to be based on negotiation as equal partners, or quasi market arrangements, rather than on conventional hierarchical control arrangements. Consequently, it is argued that the previously clearly defined vertical and lateral boundaries among elected politicians, appointed officials, public agencies and private or voluntary organisations have blurred with the diffusion of power within society.

# 3

# The Bureaucracy in India

Present chapter underlines the bureaucratic structure in India. After a systematic discussion on it, present chapter delves into analysing the role of bureaucracy from the point of view of economic development in India. Bureucratic sttructure is analysed in Section-1 and the role of bureaucracy on economic development is analysed in Section-2.

## SECION-1

### 3.1 Bureaucratic Structure in India

The Indian Administrative Service (IAS), one of the three All India Services (along with the Indian Police Service and the Indian Forest Service) plays a major role in managing the bureaucracy of both the Union Government (Central Government) and the state governments, with its officers holding strategic posts across the country. The precursor of the IAS was the Indian Civil Service (ICS) during the British Raj era. Upon independence, the new Republic of India accepted the then serving Indian Civil Service officers who chose to stay on rather than leave for the UK, and renamed the service the Indian Administrative Service. The officials of the IAS are involved in civil administration and policy-making. Like many other civil services bodies, officers of the IAS are selected by the Civil Services Examination, a three-stage a competitive selection process consisting of a preliminary exam, a main exam, and an interview. This Civil Services Examination is administered by the Union Public Service Commission once a year. After being selected for the IAS, candidates are allocated to "cadres". There is one cadre in each Indian state, except for three joint cadres: Assam-Meghalaya, Manipur-Tripura, and Arunachal Pradesh-Goa-Mizoram-Union Territories (AGMUT). The Constituent Assembly of India intended that the bureaucracy should be able to speak out freely, without fear of persecution or financial insecurity as an essential element in unifying the nation. The IAS officers are recruited by the Union government on the recommendation of the Union Public Service Commission (UPSC) and posted under various State governments. While the respective State Governments have control over them they can not censure or take disciplinary action against IAS and other All India Services officers without consulting the Union Government and the UPSC. This independence has been sometimes severely criticised by many quarters of civil society. Before India became independent, the Indian Civil Service (ICS) probationers were given general training in four British Universities of Oxford, Cambridge, London and Dublin for a period of one to two years. During the Second World War, when it was not possible to do so, a temporary training camp was organised at Dehradun. After Independence, the ICS was converted into IAS, and IAS Training School was setup in 1947 at the Metcalfe House in Delhi. It provided one year multi-purpose training to the IAS probationers. In 1957, the IAS Staff College was established at Shimla to provide a refresher training course for senior IAS officers of six to ten years of service. Both these training institutions of Delhi and Shimla were merged in 1959 to setup the National Academy of Administration at Mussoorie (Now called Lal Bahadur Sastri National Academy of Administration, LBSNAA). Since then, this academy has been imparting training to IAS probationers.

## 3.2 Progression of IAS Officers in State and Centre Government

IAS officers time scales:

- Junior Time Scale (entry-level)
- Senior Time Scale (four years of service) — equivalent to an Under Secretary to the Govt. of India.
- Junior Administrative Grade (nine years of service) — Deputy Secretaries
- Selection Grade (13 years of service) — Directors
- Joint Secretary (GOI)
- Additional Secretary (GOI)
- Secretary (GOI) — highest rank (basic pay of 80,000 Indian rupees)
- Cabinet Secretary — only one (basic pay of 90,000 Indian rupees).

The State Governments however have a kind of leverage to post these officers. Normally when an IAS officer joins the State, he is placed as a Sub Divisional Magistrate (SDM). Ideally he is to be made in charge of a District after completing 9 years of service and entering the Junior Administrative Grade but in certain States, even younger IAS officers are made in charge of Districts (Known as District Magistrates (DM), Deputy Commissioners (DCs or Collectors), like in Uttar Pradesh 4 year senior officer may be appointed as D.M. The hierarchy of IAS officers at the Government of India and state Government level is shown in the following table 3.1. As discernable from this table, it takes longer time to achieve equivalent positions at the centre due to lack of vacancies and slower rate of promotions.

**Table 3.1**

| *Sl No* | *Positions in the Government of India* | *Equivalent Position in the State Government* |
|---|---|---|
| 1 | Under Secretary(4) | Deputy Secretary/Additional District Magistrate(Entry Level) |
| 2 | Deputy Secretary(9) | Joint Secretary/ District Magist- |

| | | |
|---|---|---|
| | | rate/Deputy Commissioner(6) |
| 3 | Director(12) | Special Secretary, Heads of Departments(9) |
| 4 | Joint secretary(20) | Secretary(16) |
| 5 | Additional Secretary(30) | Principal Secretaries/Financial Commissioners(24) |
| 6 | Secretary(34) | Chief Secretary(30) |
| 7 | Cabinet Secretary | No Equivalent (Constitutional Authority-ranked 11th in the table of Precedence) |

N:B: 1. Figures in the brackets indicate minimum years in the IAS to achieve said designation, though not the only criteria.

## SECTION-2

### 3.3 Role of Bureaucracy on Economic Development

Economic theories of development have multiplied since the 1950s, providing material for a prolific branch of economics in which discussion is rife. Each of these theories has its own view of the role of the state in development processes. The object of this Chapter is to analyse this aspect of the economic theory of development, applying a political sociology of the 'developing states' which has the advantage of a bird's-eye view of their historical evolution over the past forty years. It is shown that economic development theory has continually propagated 'myths' of the state. Three of these are analysed in succession: the myth of the 'developer state' in economic take-off theories (1950s-1960s), the myth of the 'puppet state' in pendency theories (the 1970s), and the myth of the 'small-scale liberal state' in neo-classical theory (1980s-1990s) [Franck Petiteville (1998)].

Economic development theory is a branch of economics which has progressed by leaps and bounds since the 1950s. At that time, decolonization, the emergence of the new Third World states and the concomitant extension of the industrial age throughout the world led to a 'demand' for speedier economic development, with the result that economics, too, was very much in demand and assumed greater importance in both the academic field and in the international agencies

(World Bank, IMF, UNDP, UNIDO, UNCTAD, etc.) than previously. This economic development theory, which generated operational 'development policies' for the states of the South, was therefore highly prescriptive by its very nature. The object of this article is to identify the concept of the state conveyed by economic development theory. With the help of political science, an attempt will be made to understand how economic theories of development have often failed to take account of the complexity of the 'state factor'. Discussion of the merits and demerits of the various economic policies put forward by development theorists will be left to the economists. This article will simply review the assumptions underlying these theories in regard to the nature of the developing states, and assess them in the light of a political science which has the advantage of a bird's eye view of the historical evolution of these states.

There will of course be no question of affirming the superiority of political science over economics: from the 1950s to the 1970s political science, too, indulged in the pleasure of building up ambitious 'political development' theories with defects (normativeness, ethnocentricity, and evolutionism) similar in many respects to those frequently attributed to economic theories of development (Badie, 1994). However, it is precisely because the sociological approach to the developing states has now sloughed off the perverse effects of developmentalist theorizing that it is attempting to contribute to the current reappraisal of the economic theories of development from the point of view of the state, comparing economic theories of the state with sociological and historical reality in the 'developing states'. For the benefit of readers who are not economists, the main economic theories of development put forward since the 1950s are reviewed here in summary form. (In order to keep to a select bibliography, the many studies in which these theories are set forth are not mentioned here. They can easily be found, however, in any good survey of economic development theory, for example in Oman and Wignaraja, 1991.) These theories will be grouped under three heads: the 'economic take-off theories elaborated in the 1950s and 1960s, the critical theories of 'dependency' constructed in the 1970s, and finally the neoclassical theory of development which has triumphed over the two preceding trends. These three types of development theory have produced particular concepts of the status and role of the state which will be examined in turn. The myth of the 'developer state' in economic take-off theories (1950s-1960s): an economistic reduction of the developing state The first great economic development theories formulated in the 1950s advocated, on the lines of the Marshall Plan, big international transfers of funds to the Third World states to enable them to accumulate the capital required for a level of investment regarded as decisive for setting in motion a process of rapid industrial modernization. Western development economists expected these massive injections of funds to break 'the vicious circle of poverty' (Ragnar Nurkse's theory), to speed up a massive migration of labour from agriculture to industry (the Arthur Lewis model), to spark off the 'big push' of industrial growth (Paul Rosenstein-Rodan's theory) and, more generally, to launch the global 'take-off' of society for the industrial age (the third stage in W.W. Rostow's famous five-stage development theory). Whereas most of these liberal economists from the English-speaking world confined the role of the state to the efficient distribution of investment in an open economy, Information Integrity. Less orthodox writers in Europe recommended increased intervention of the state in a protected industrial sector. The key was for the Third World states to favour voluntaristic, selective public investment in the industrial sectors regarded as the most strategic in terms of spin-off for the economy. The expressions then used were: leading sector (Albert Hirschman), growth poles (Francois Perroux) and industrializing industries (Gerard de Bernis). As for the attitude to be adopted to the world market, this planned industrial development was seen most of the time as a means of securing the home market through import-substitution policies (influence of the Raul Prebisch's thesis). Tending towards interventionism tinged with socialist planning, an economist such as Paul Baran went so far as to advocate that the state appropriate and turn to account the potential 'economic surplus' of underdeveloped economies (land and mineral resources, foreign investments) by means of a vigorous policy of nationalization of these strategic productive sectors. Other more unorthodox writers, such as the Swedish Social Democrat Gunnar Myrdal, prematurely anxious to convert economic growth into equitable social development, appealed for the emergence in the Third World of redistributive states on the lines of the welfare states appearing in the West.

The most interventionist strategies quickly found favour with the Third World states—at all events, the states with most influence on the ideological leadership of the non-aligned countries. Algeria's economic planning was thus to take inspiration from the industrializing industries theory. An Indian version of this theory (the Mahalanobis growth model) served as a basis for India's Second Five-Year Plan (1956-1961), while in the Middle East, nationalization of mineral resources, and even of Western interests (the Suez Canal), spread from one state to the other. In Latin America, ECLAC supported import-substitution strategies. Although all the economists responsible for these development theories can be contrasted with one another, as much on account of their ideas as of their educational backgrounds (English-speaking liberals such as Lewis or Rostow and unorthodox French writers such as Perroux or De Bernis are worlds apart), it is not too extreme a simplification to say that the economic development theories of the 1950s-1960s were, as a whole, based on a concept of the Third World states as having a Promethean capacity for economic and social development via rapid industrial modernization. The desire of the state elites in the Third World to promote development went without question and was seen as being able to solve the question of socio-economic development without any political problem. The liberal economists were not excessively concerned about the absence of immediate social spin-off from growth in the countries which followed a development strategy in line with their ideas, convinced as they were — by Simon Kuznets' very persuasive hypothesis — that the first stage of development would end with an increase in social inequalities, after which 'trickle-down' mechanisms would have a redistributive effect. The more unorthodox writers, meanwhile, seemed to have absolute confidence in the progressive' aims of the state elites in the Third World who were putting their ideas into practice. Francois Perroux wrote in 1962 that it was sufficient to create elites capable of assuming the interests of a number of nations and serving their interests, bearing in mind that the historical expansion of industry demonstrates its rational purpose, which is to serve everyone (Perroux, 1962, p. 228). The Swede Gunnar Myrdal, alone, perhaps, in the community of development economists, expressed some scepticism, asking whether the very nature of the Third World states might not be an obstacle to development. In fact he repeatedly stressed the likelihood of states being too 'lax' to undertake efficient development policies or too authoritarian or too corrupt to carry out policies liable to redistribute the fruits of growth. However, his warning voice was drowned in the optimism of the time, and above all in the prevailing economism, which excluded this type of political conjecture from the economic field. In defining the debate on the state in the developing countries in these terms, the economists were being flagrantly ethnocentric, projecting categories of economic analysis specific to contemporary Western states onto political entities which, in many cases, had nothing in common with them except the formal title of state and, in recent times, representation at the United Nations. To be more precise, crediting the Third World 'states' with a Promethean capacity for developing their economies and their respective societies was the combined result of a considerable verestimation of the economic factor, serious neglect of the historicity of the relationship of the state to the economy and to society, and failure to analyse not only the state's development resources but also its mode of operation. Professional bias and the all-pervasive ethnocentrism of the time made most of the economists of the 1950s-1960s quite confident of the universality of the Western cultural model of technical/ economic accumulation and of the dominance of this process of accumulation in any process Information Integrity of overall social change. This fundamental twofold negation of the indissociably cultural nature of economic processes and of the pluri-dimensional nature of social change is generally recognized by economists nowadays as an initial flaw in development theory. What is more, the development theories of the 1950s-1960s were ethnocentric in a rather short-sighted way, being more influenced by the interventionist model of the modernizing state inherited from Keynes, the New Deal and the emerging state planning approach than by the constitution over the centuries of relations of differentiation and interaction between the Western state and its economy and society. This long-term view is highlighted by all the historical and historico-sociological studies on the formation of the modern state in Europe (Badie and Birnbaum, 1982). As pointed out by Jean-Francois Bayart, following in the footsteps of Fernand Braudel, the assumption that efficient 'developer' states would emerge in the newly independent Third World countries, as a result of the colonial heritage of the 'civilizing' state and the influence of contemporary Western states, failed to take account of the time factor in the context of Third World countries, that is, the long period required to establish some historical basis for the relationship between state, economy and society (Bayart, 1996). The mistake was aggravated in this case by the flagrant underestimation of the disparity between the Promethean development mission assigned to the states of the South and the meagre resources available to them in terms of public policy as compared with the magnitude of the socio-economic tasks involved (one has only to think of the challenges of population planning or schooling for the population as a whole). In short, economic development theory attributed to states which in many cases were not really states at all a role in overall development which no Western state had ever had to assume as a matter of urgency or on such a huge scale. These two forms of bias led economists to postulate, rather hastily, the existence of states constituted according to the Western legal/rational model and differentiated from the economic sphere to the extent of being able to frame economic policies meeting strict economic criteria. We realize now that in many Third World states this was not the case. The interpenetration of the political and economic elites did not always enable the states to set up genuine development strategies. It was only very much later that it was realized that the strategies of the elites were not necessarily conducive to economic development. The example of Africa was conclusive. There this interpenetration of the political and economic elites hinged on the use of the bureaucratic apparatus of the state by the politico-administrative elites for the purpose of controlling a largely nationalized modern economic sector (Bakary, 1990).

The task of development and modernization in the third world country like India is not possible without a well organized and effective bureaucracy. Interest in bureaucracy and its relation to democracy predates the advent of sociology as a discipline. The bureaucratic problem is somewhat complex in developing countries where social and political institutions are relatively less developed and where the State has mainly to depend upon the administrative structure for the accomplishment of its goals. In India, development and local self-government have a long history. The Indian society which we find today is definitely not the same as it was during the British rule. It is not easy that the areas which remained sick for such a long period should regain their health so soon. All the same, the change that has taken place with in a period of 60 years is highly encouraging and laudable. Majority of the people live in rural areas in developing countries, Therefore, any attempt at bringing overall development must lay greater emphasis on rural development which is sought to be brought about through planning. The government in such countries is facing the problem of initiating and accelerating the pace of development to enhance the standard of living of the people. Bureaucracy occupies an important position in the formulation and implementation of these plans. Hence, the success or failure of development efforts to a larger extent depends upon the role performed by bureaucracy in developing countries.

After Second World War, interest in development had been witnessed not only in the third world but all over the world. Development has affected every branch of knowledge like industry, technology, education and agriculture. Naturally, much of the leadership in development has come from governmental agencies, be they international, national, State regional or local also. Perhaps the most important problem of India in particular is that of improving the economic and social conditions of people who live below poverty line.

They include our society's landless labourers, small and marginal farmers, artisans and other weaker sections. In fact there are no two opinions about the need of development wherein the role of bureaucracy is both important as well as essential. But there is no empirical evidence to highlight the deficiencies which creep into any system or every system despite the best efforts of all concerned. The fact that nearly 75 per cent of the total population of India dwells in the villages, it would be worthwhile to focus attention on the role of bureaucracy in the development. The proposed study is one of the first of its kind as an appraisal of the role of bureaucracy in the development.

This research study concerns with the structural and behavioural aspects of bureaucracy in rural development. The major focus of attention of researchers of Indian bureaucracy had been on the Indian Civil Services and its successors i.e. the Indian Administrative Services. Lower ranks of bureaucracy had received scant attention.1 We acknowledge its (IAS) importance in the total political system but we feel it is more important to turn our attention to those bureaucrats who are easily identified with development efforts of the State and are actively involved in eliciting public cooperation for development tasks. In this research study, efforts are directed towards not only the bureaucracy at secretariat and district levels but also at the block level which is engaged in implementing the rural development programmes. This section of bureaucracy has certainly a great contemporary relevance in the overall development of India in general and Bihar in particular. The functionaries at the lower level are the Block Development Officers, Extension Officers and Village Level Workers (VLW). They are the government officials who interact with the people, mould and influence public attitudes towards development in a significant way. It is also at the local level that the hardest core of traditions and beliefs are found and policies undergo their most severe test for implementation.

Therefore, to provide immediate relevance and a contemporary understanding in the context of development, State level bureaucracy for policy making and District and Block level Bureaucracy for implementing the policy and programmes has been selected. Rural development programme is the single most of important vehicle of government, initiated for purpose of socio-economic uplift. The government has devoted great attention to this aspect of change. The present study focuses its attention on the bureaucratic behaviour and its performance in the execution of development projects.

After the initiation of community development and Panchayati Raj, the development scene tended to highlight the relations between political leaders and administrators also. It was argued that the successor of local institutions as instruments of development rested on the ability of the political and administrative leadership to cooperate with one another and resolve the tensions and conflicts arising from the social environment. The administrative machinery set up for community development programme soon gave way to the three-tier Panchayati Raj system in order to make rural development administration responsive to the elected representatives of the people. The block was recognised as the focal point of planning and administration and it became the single most important unit of both community development as well as Panchayati Raj. It is because of this reason that the study of bureaucracy both at the secretariat and grass root level has been taken up. There is abundant literature on "Bureaucracy and Development". A large number of studies have been conducted pertaining to the various aspects of bureaucracy and development in India and other countries of the world. Other than the Indian Scholars on bureaucracy, there are some foreign observers on the subject who had studied the bureaucracy in depth. Paul Appleby, F.W. Riggs, Ralph Brainbanti, La Palombara, Hugh Tinker, Ursula Hicks, and David Potter ere some of them. Some of the notable Indian Scholars who have done researches on Bureaucracy and Development are Kuldeep Mathur (*Bureaucratic Response to Development* 1973), (*Bureaucracy and New Agricultural Strategy* 1983). C.P. Bhambhri (*Bureaucracy and Politics in India* 1971). R.B. Jain and P.N. Chaudhuri (*Bureaucratic Values in Development* 1982). G. Mare Gopal (*Administrative Leadership and Rural Development in India* 1980). H.R. Chaturvedi (*Bureaucracy and Local Community Dynamics of Rural Development* 1977). A. Avasthi and Romesh Arora (*Bureaucracy and Development: Indian Perspectives* 1978). P.R. Dubhashi: (*Rural Development Administration in India*). S.R. Maheshwari (*Rural Development in India* 1985). L.C. Jain &. B.V. Krishnamurthy, P.M. Tripathi (*Grass without Roots: Rural Development Under Government Auspices* 1985). After mentioning the various studies on this aspect, it can be said that lot of studies in this field have been done in various States of the country but very little has been done in Bihar.

The developing countries directed their efforts towards economic, social and political development after attaining independence from colonial rule. In the modern age every democratic government has to face gigantic task of all round development. Though the concept of development administration is of recent origin but has become quite popular and a fashionable expression in administrative parlance. Development needed to be conceived as a dynamic process directed towards transforming the entire society embarking together its economic, social, political and administrative aspects for an all around balance upward change. Development administrations is thus that aspect of public administration that focuses on government influenced change towards progressive political, economic and social objectives According to Weinder, development is a State of mind, a tendency, a direction, rather than a fixed goal, it is a rate of change in a particular direction. The task of nation-building and bringing about major socio-economic changes in the under developed and developing world is the main theme behind the concept of development administration.

Again the importance of development within the broad framework of development administration is of utmost necessity in the modern world. The concept of development was viewed differently by different scholars as it was completely a new concept for third world countries. But as a whole development is not a new concept. Several pioneering experiments have been made in this direction by many eminent scholars and practitioners. The concept of what is known as development was born in the context of agriculture, and it remained for long time, coterminus with agriculture development in India. The Royal Commission on Agriculture

(1928), for instance provides this kind of interpretation to rural development. Agriculture is at the heart but not the whole development, Planning Commission Task Force on Integrated Rural Development observed in 1972 also observed likewise.

Now we have decided to take what might be considered a rather restricted view of the expression 'development'. We have chosen to equate it with agricultural development in the widest sense so as to embrace, besides crop husbandry, all the allied activities. Development has meant the extension of irrigation facilities, expansion of electricity, improvement in the techniques of cultivation, construction of school buildings and the provision of educational facilities, health care etc.

Development since seventies in general has began to be viewed in terms of the contribution it makes to the reduction of poverty, inequality and exploitation. Development reflects these concerns and is manifested in special programmes for the weaker sections of the community and backward areas. Developments in content and form is concerned with multi sectoral programmes involving development in productive agriculture and its related services, industrial activities, transportation, communication and infrastructures, health and education services etc.

After seventies, the concept of development has become, more confining in its interpretation. The World Bank boldly marks such a shift in emphasis and defines development as a strategy designed to improve the economic and social life of a specific group of people — the poor. It involves extending the benefits of development to the poorest among those who seek a livelihood in the underdeveloped areas. The group includes small scale farmers, tenants and landless. The SFDA, MFAL, NREP, IRIP, DPAP and minimum needs programmes have become too well known and are part of India's new Twenty Point Programme. In order to appreciate the new concept of development, it is necessary to note what was felt to be unsatisfactory in some of the earlier approaches. With out wishing over simplify or over generalise issues of policy and problems of implementation which are by no means uniform country to country or even area to area in a given country. Some of the new concepts and objectives in rural development are related to the above set of considerations and have the professed objective of remedying such lacunae. The current approaches to development thus emphasize the following:

> Our development system can be analyzed in terms of three inter related aspects of rural communities. They are: (a) individual member of the community, (b) organisational aspects, and (c) the environment of the rural community. In accordance with strategies of stimulation and inducement of rural development, therefore, government should encourage changes in individual aspects regarding their perceptions and of motivation attitudes, world outlook and skills and knowledge required for development. Government should also induce organizational change in rural communities in terms of leadership structure made of people's participation and institutional linkages.

The third important concern of policy makers will be how to provide a sufficient level of environment support in terms of political leadership commitment, supportive policy measures, political and administrative framework, and other social and economic supporting linkages.

In a country like ours, where majority of the vast population actually live and work in villages, the task relating to rural development acquires special importance. National development is inconceivable and impossible without rural development. According to 1981 Census, 78 percent of India's population (680 million) lives in villages while there are not more than 3,000 cities and towns. 40 per cent of rural population is estimated to live below poverty line as against 41 per cent in urban areas. Foreign rulers paid little attention to the development of India and only confined to limited function of collecting land revenue and maintaining law and order which helped the British to improve the British economy. It was only after independence that with the transfer of political power to Indians, a serious thought was given to development of the people.

Therefore, the first and foremost challenge to the Indian administrative system of independent India was how to meet the socio economic needs of these rural poor. This can possibly be with the introduction of rural development programmes for the rural India. Rural development is advocated today as basic strategy for economic development all over the world and India is no exception. The sheer largeness in Numbers Who continue to live and work in the rural areas in the developing countries, particularly India, the biggest democracy of the world, compels our attention to this important yet neglected sector of the economy. The idea of rural development originated by Mahatma Gandhi in his teachings was the champion of Gram Raj. Gandhiji succeeded in mobilising the poor people from the villages in the unique battle for freedom by holding out before them the prospectus of better life, more dignity and honour.

Due to the absence of popular local institutions, in the beginning, the responsibility of implementation of the community development programmes was given to the steel frame bureaucracy in India. The bureaucracy failed to inspire the people's cooperation in community development programme due to its rigid approach, conservatism and lack of development attitude. As a result of its failure, on the recommendation or Balwant Rai Mehta Team, Government of India recommended the decentralization of power and authority to the popular local institution i.e. Panchayati Raj institutions. In the opinion of Late Pandit Jawahar Lal Nehru both officials and non-officials and their part to play in the community development work.

"In India the question of development was initiated with community development programme in fifties, then in sixties the area development programme was launched, in seventies integrated rural development programme become popular and the latest emphasis now on the individual development programme realized to uplift the poorest from the level of poverty to better living".

# 4

# Status of Economic Development in Orissa

The economy of Orissa has been lagging behind the national economy by several decades. Its per capita net state domestic product, a measure of average income, stood at Rs. 20200 for 2006-07 which falls behind the national average by about 35 per cent. Moreover, the gross domestic product of the state grew by a considerable lower rate than many other states for a long time despite its high growth potential. Drawing on the experience of several countries as well as that of India, various studies concluded that economic growth was the most critical factor for reduction of incidence of poverty in the state. On the poverty dimension, the recent developments have been gloomy, to say the least. The consumption expenditure surveys carried out by the National Sample Survey Organisation (NSSO), the standard source of data for poverty analysis in India by official and non-official investigators, shows that the period 1993-2004 has witnessed a reversal of the achievements made on the poverty front during 1983-93. The prima facie evidence points towards a case of growth without inclusion and needs further probe. To provide the reader with a quick background, we may briefly note that movement in poverty is affected by two factors: (a) growth in mean income or consumption, and

(b) change in distribution parameter. Low per capita income growth along with near invariance of the distribution parameter led to little improvement in level of living of the poor in India for about three decades after independence. Incidence of poverty started to fall after mid-1970s at the all-India level when the economy moved to a high growth phase of above 5% per annum. In view of this and similar experience for other countries, generally agreed that 3 economic growth is an essential precondition for poverty reduction. Examining the India data over several decades, Ravallion and Datt (1996) showed that growth in mean consumption accounted for as much as 80% of the cumulative decline in poverty in India. Based on cross-country experience, international organizations such as the World Bank and the Asian Development Bank have often found that income elasticity of poverty lies between 1.5 to 2.0, meaning thereby a given growth in aggregate per capita income can reduce poverty more than proportionately. Such partial elasticity estimates assumes constancy of income distribution which may not hold in practice for a specific country. After the reforms process started in 1991, India has of course witnessed higher economic growth but rate of poverty reduction has not been faster. The income elasticity of poverty in India seems to have reduced to 0.4 between 1993-94 and 2004-05 (Panda, 2008). In order to make the Indian growth process more broad based, the Planning Commission (2008) has recently advocated measures for 'inclusive growth'. Against the above background, it is a matter of concern that some key indicators for Orissa point towards a process of growth without inclusion. While uneven regional growth remains alarmingly high and probably increasing in the country, many rural areas received a setback in the 1990s, especially in backward states and in terms of employment, agricultural growth and poverty reduction. Several studies have observed that the disparity in regional growth has widened in India during post-reformed period (Ahluwalia, 2000, 2003; Rao, Shand and Kalirajan 1999; Shand and Bhide 2000; Bhattacharya and Saktivel 2004). However, some poor states, where sizeable proportion of total people live in rural areas, have little different experience in terms of income, poverty, employment and quality of live over period. The fact that the four poor states— Bihar, Uttar Pradesh, Madhya Pradesh and Orrisa together have 55% of all people living below the poverty line. While some states have experienced benefits of economic liberalization in 1990s, poor states like Orissa suffered major setback particularly in rural areas in terms of employment, poverty, agriculture and overall growth, which is grossly reflected in terms of human development. This is despite of several special packages exclusively designed for rural areas and backward areas to accelerate rural growth process. On the other hand, given the approximately similar initial conditions and constraints, some states have performed better. This chapter covers three sections. In the first section, the incidence, depth and severity of poverty of Orissa is discussed considering its historic and spatial dimensions. Occupation wise, social class wise distribution of the incidence of poverty is also discussed. In the second section, the situation of food security in Orissa is discussed in the light of food availability at the regional level as well as at the household level. The access to food at household level is analysed considering the available secondary information based on the anthropometric indicators, clinical observations, and calorie shortfall groups. In the final section the scenario of employment and agriculture is presented.

## Poverty Measurement in Orissa

In Orissa, two types of data sources are available on the extent of poverty. The first one is related with the estimation of poverty by using unit record data of NSSO on consumption expenditure. The second one concerns the income method as adopted by Panchayatiraj Department, (Govt. of Orissa) by conducting socio-economic survey of households. As per this method people below Rs.11000 are treated as poverty stricken people.

## Incidence of Poverty in Orissa

Analysis of 55th round consumer expenditure data of NSSO (1999-2000) indicates that Orissa is the poorest among all the states followed by Bihar. In comparison to previous NSS round (50th round) in 1993-94, there has been marginal decline in the incidence of rural poverty from 49.80 to 47.8 percent in Orissa. Among the BPL population in Orissa, the share of moderately poor, very poor and extremely poor people stand at 26.1, 21.7 and 2.8 percent respectively. The adjoining State AP is much better off than Orissa, where only about 10 percent of the people are below the poverty line (Radhakrishna, Rao, Ravi & Reddy 2004). The incidence of urban poverty in Orissa in comparison to all other States is as high as 43.5 percent of the urban population. However, 90 percent of poor people in Orissa reside in rural areas and only 9.7 percent of the poor people are living in urban areas (Report of the Expert Group on Estimation of Proportion and Number of the Poor 1993). Thus, poverty in Orissa is very much a rural phenomenon.

**Table 4.1: Incidence of Rural Poverty in Orissa in Comparison to other States and All India at two Time Periods**

| *Sl. No.* | *All India/States* | *Percentage of BPL population to total population 1993-94* | *Percentage of BPL population to total population in 1999-00* |
|---|---|---|---|
| 1 | All India | 36.8 | 26.5 |
| 2 | Andhra Pradesh | 15.9 | 10.5 |
| 3 | Arunachal Pradesh | 41.4 | 23.4 |
| 4 | Assam | 45.3 | 40.2 |
| 5 | Bihar | 44.3 | 44.0 |
| 6 | Goa | 5.0 | 0.0 |
| 7 | Gujarat | 22.1 | 12.4 |
| 8 | Haryana | 28.3 | 7.4 |
| 9 | Himachal Pradesh | 30.3 | 7.5 |
| 10 | Jammu & Kashmir | 18.2 | 4.7 |
| 11 | Karnataka | 30.2 | 16.9 |
| 12 | Kerala | 25.4 | 9.4 |
| 13 | Madhya Pradesh | 40.7 | 37.2 |
| 14 | Maharastra | 37.9 | 23.3 |
| 15 | Manipur | 19.2 | 14.1 |
| 16 | Meghalaya | 24.3 | 6.0 |
| 17 | Mizoram | 6.2 | 2.8 |
| 18 | Nagaland | 1.9 | 0.2 |

| | | | |
|---|---|---|---|
| 19 | Orissa | 49.8 | 47.8 |
| 20 | Punjab | 11.7 | 6.0 |
| 21 | Rajasthan | 26.4 | 13.4 |
| 22 | Sikkim | 31.3 | 21.7 |
| 23 | Tamilnadu | 33.0 | 20.1 |
| 24 | Tripura | 23.3 | 16.7 |
| 25 | Uttar Pradesh | 42.4 | 31.0 |
| 26 | West Bengal | 41.2 | 31.7 |

*Source:*· Economics Survey, Ministry of Finance, Government of India (2001).

In the year 1960-61, Orissa and Andhra Pradesh were almost on the similar pattern so far as the rural poverty in the two states are concerned. In this year, the incidence of poverty in Orissa and Andhra Pradesh was 48.34 and 46.82 respectively. After 40 years, Andhra Pradesh has been able to reduce its poverty to 11.05%, whereas, Orissa's position remains the same as it was in the year 1960-61. Year-by-year, the gap in the trend line of incidence of poverty in Orissa [$Y=63.681+(-0.6029)x$; $R^2=0.1272$] and Andhra Pradesh [$Y=+55919+(-2.322)x$; $R^2 = 0.735$] it getting widened. The incidence of poverty, in Orissa, tends to increase up to the year 1968-69, until it culminates at 70.25 percent. Only except a marginal decline in the year 1970-71 it tends to increase and for the subsequent years, there have been continuous fluctuations. Over the years, the rate of decline in poverty trend is very slog against a secular decline in the poverty trend of Andhra Pradesh (see Table 4.2 and Fig. 4.1).

**Table 4.2: Proportion of Rural Population Below Poverty Line in Orissa and Andhra Pradesh**

| *Sl.No.* | *Years* | *Orissa* | *Andhra Pradesh* |
|---|---|---|---|
| 1 | 1961-62 | 48.34 | 46.82 |
| 2 | 1963-64 | 59.02 | 44.60 |
| 3 | 1964-65 | 60.68 | 40.92 |
| 4 | 1965-66 | 61.66 | 44.21 |
| 5 | 1966-67 | 64.50 | 49.44 |
| 6 | 1967-68 | 63.89 | 48.42 |
| 7 | 1968-69 | 70.25 | 45.02 |
| 8 | 1969-70 | 65.94 | 44.95 |

| 9 | 1970-71 | 60.51 | 40.00 |
|---|---|---|---|
| 10 | 1972-73 | 66.07 | 42.00 |
| 11 | 1973-74 | 57.98 | 37.75 |
| 12 | 1977-78 | 61.49 | 30.21 |
| 13 | 1986-87 | 40.13 | 16.60 |
| 14 | 1987-88 | 58.70 | 21.00 |
| 15 | 1993-94 | 49.72 | 15.92 |
| 16 | 1999-00 | 48.01 | 11.05 |

*Source:* Dev (1988), Malhotra (1997), Deaton (2003).

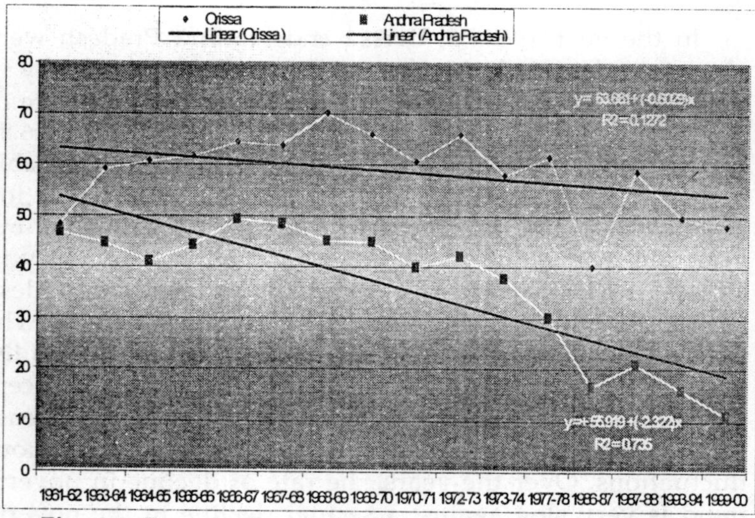


**Fig. 4.1: Poverty Trends in Orissa and Andhra Pradesh**

## Inter-District Variation in Poverty

On the basis of different income groups to study the inter-district variation of poverty, the BPL households are classified into Destitutes, Very Very Poor, Very Poor and Poor households for the income groups like Rs. 0-4000, 4001-6000, 6001-8500, 8501-11000 per annum respectively. It is found from Table 4.3 that in five districts where high incidence of BPL households are noticed include—Phulbani, Malkangiri, Bolangir, Gajapati and Nabarangapur. It is to note that even though the districts like Phulbani and Gajapati are not coming under KBK districts, but these districts are bordering to KBK districts. It is to be mentioned that the incidence of poverty is more serious in and around the KBK districts. Phulbani has the highest proportion of BPL households (93.03), but Rayagada and Koraput, even though coming under KBK have comparatively lower proportion of BPL households. Mayurbhanj, another tribal dominated district outside the KBK region has very high proportion of BPL households (90.77%). It is remarkable to note that Phulbani has the highest proportion (42.22%) of destitute among all the districts of Orissa. Thus, Phulbani needs special attention.

**Table 4.3: District-wise Distribution of Rural Families Below Poverty Line on the Basis of Different Income Groups (in Percentage Terms)**

| *Sl. No.* | *Name of the District* | *0-4000 (Destitute)* | *4001-6000 (Very very poor)* | *6001-8500 (Very poor)* | *8501-11000 (poor)* | *Total* |
|---|---|---|---|---|---|---|
| 1 | Angul | 32.60 | 32.02 | 14.68 | 5.04 | 84.34 |
| 2 | Balasore | 24.94 | 25.67 | 10.25 | 4.10 | 64.29 |
| 3 | Bargarh | 21.38 | 27.84 | 13.78 | 6.95 | 69.96 |
| 4 | Bhadrak | 20.12 | 28.76 | 15.22 | 7.06 | 71.16 |
| 5 | Bolangir | 25.67 | 34.46 | 22.44 | 9.32 | 91.90 |
| 6 | Cuttack | 17.59 | 27.53 | 15.71 | 10.94 | 71.77 |
| 7 | Dhenkanal | 28.90 | 34.66 | 14.64 | 5.98 | 84.17 |
| 8 | Gajapati | 33.32 | 35.43 | 17.53 | 5.23 | 91.51 |
| 9 | Ganjam | 29.19 | 24.67 | 14.19 | 7.15 | 75.20 |
| 10 | Jagatsingpur | 21.61 | 20.95 | 14.97 | 12.03 | 69.57 |
| 11 | Jajpur | 21.92 | 23.86 | 15.73 | 10.35 | 71.87 |
| 12 | Kalahandi | 27.78 | 35.51 | 16.83 | 6.65 | 86.77 |
| 13 | Kendrapara | 17.23 | 24.91 | 15.83 | 11.34 | 69.31 |
| 14 | Kendujhar | 27.62 | 29.59 | 17.60 | 8.14 | 82.95 |
| 15 | Khurda | 21.18 | 35.06 | 14.12 | 5.55 | 75.91 |
| 16 | Koraput | 24.16 | 35.92 | 18.40 | 8.10 | 86.59 |
| 17 | Malkangiri | 30.82 | 36.51 | 16.93 | 7.60 | 91.86 |
| 18 | Mayurbhanj | 34.76 | 35.65 | 15.00 | 5.36 | 90.77 |
| 19 | Nuapada | 24.52 | 32.56 | 20.96 | 8.28 | 86.32 |
| 20 | Nabarangpur | 33.56 | 33.38 | 16.89 | 6.73 | 90.05 |
| 21 | Nayagada | 24.96 | 38.36 | 15.14 | 5.08 | 83.54 |
| 22 | Puri | 23.38 | 26.01 | 17.05 | 8.22 | 74.69 |
| 23 | Rayagada | 29.16 | 28.88 | 17.35 | 6.16 | 81.56 |

| | | | | | | |
|---|---|---|---|---|---|---|
| 24 | Sonepur | 28.07 | 25.03 | 9.75 | 4.60 | 67.44 |
| 25 | Sundargarh | 22.58 | 31.28 | 18.34 | 8.72 | 80.93 |
| 26 | Phulbani | 42.22 | 34.16 | 12.59 | 4.06 | 93.03 |
| 27 | Boudh | 19.50 | 37.43 | 19.95 | 8.32 | 85.20 |
| 28 | Sambalpur | 24.21 | 24.78 | 12.27 | 4.50 | 65.63 |
| 29 | Deogarh | 29.66 | 30.27 | 12.57 | 6.29 | 78.49 |
| 30 | Jharsuguda | 15.24 | 21.90 | 15.55 | 3.96 | 63.67 |
| | ALL ORISSA | 25.89 | 30.01 | 15.55 | 7.24 | 78.70 |

*Source:* Panchayatiraj Department (1992), Govt. of Orissa.

## Regional Differences of Poverty within Orissa

The National Sample Survey on the basis of agro-climatic zones has divided Orissa into three zones — coastal, southern, and northern zones. Coastal zones include Ganjam, Puri, Cuttack and Balasore; Southern zones include Phulbani, Koraput and Kalahandi and Northern zones include Bolangir, Dhenkanal, Sundargarh, Sambalpur, Kendujhar and Mayurbhanj. These entire districts are undivided districts. The regional differences in poverty as per the estimates of Hann and Dubey (2003) based upon during last four NSS rounds is presented in Table 4.4.

**Table 4.4: Regional Differences in Poverty During Different NSS Rounds**

| *Rural* | *Official Poverty Line* | | | | *International ($/ a day) poverty line* | | | |
|---|---|---|---|---|---|---|---|---|
| | *Coastal* | *Southern* | *Northern* | *Orissa* | *Coastal* | *Southern* | *Northern* | *Orissa* |
| 1 | 2 | 3 | 4 | 5 | 6 | 7 | 8 | 9 |
| *Rural* | | | | | | | | |
| 1983 | 57.97 | 80.76 | 75.22 | 68.43 | 47.57 | 75.93 | 68.64 | 60.46 |
| 1987-88 | 48.37 | 82.98 | 61.01 | 58.62 | 55.33 | 85.61 | 65.49 | 63.98 |
| 1993-94 | 45.33 | 68.84 | 45.82 | 49.80 | 66.71 | 83.85 | 62.51 | 68.40 |
| 1999-00 | 29.30 | 86.16 | 50.98 | 48.13 | 47.85 | 92.70 | 66.98 | 63.44 |
| *Urban* | | | | | | | | |
| 1983 | 46.15 | 45.48 | 54.35 | 49.66 | 24.84 | 27.84 | 33.55 | 28.84 |
| 1987-88 | 42.11 | 52.93 | 39.90 | 42.58 | 22.64 | 29.71 | 25.59 | 24.74 |
| 1993-94 | 47.24 | 41.94 | 32.54 | 40.68 | 29.44 | 35.84 | 16.08 | 25.09 |

| | | | | | | | | |
|---|---|---|---|---|---|---|---|---|
| 1999-00 | 41.65 | 43.97 | 45.81 | 43.51 | 25.26 | 30.01 | 24.65 | 25.64 |
| *Total* | | | | | | | | |
| 1983 | 56.49 | 79.08 | 72.28 | 66.24 | 44.74 | 73.65 | 63.70 | 56.77 |
| 1987-88 | 47.67 | 80.29 | 58.16 | 56.75 | 51.67 | 80.62 | 60.10 | 59.42 |
| 1993-94 | 45.57 | 66.07 | 43.92 | 48.64 | 62.06 | 78.91 | 55.86 | 62.88 |
| 1999-00 | 31.51 | 81.27 | 50.10 | 47.37 | 43.81 | 85.46 | 59.81 | 57.24 |

*Source:* Hann and Dubey (2003) Poverty in Orissa : Divergent Trends, *Economic and Political Weekly,* 25-31, January.

## Incidence of Poverty

The estimates of incidence of poverty as per official poverty line as well as International ($/a day) poverty line reveals that the southern region is the poorest in Orissa having more than 80 percent rural people below the poverty line, whereas this proportion is around 51% for the northern region and only 29.3% for the coastal region in 1999-00. It is remarkable that in coastal Orissa rural poverty has continued to decline at a similar pace as the all India average. These estimates suggest dramatic regional divergence of poverty in Orissa (Pradhan 2005, Panda 2002).

**Table 4.5: Poverty Ratio by Social Groups in Orissa 1983 to 1999-2000**

| *Social Groups* | *Years* | | | |
|---|---|---|---|---|
| | *1983* | *1987-88* | *1993-94* | *1999-00* |
| *Orissa* | | | | |
| ST | 87.08 | 83.82 | 71.31 | 73.08 |
| SC | 75.99 | 65.75 | 49.79 | 52.30 |
| Others | 58.52 | 47.31 | 40.18 | 33.29 |
| All | 68.43 | 58.62 | 49.79 | 48.04 |
| *All India* | | | | |
| ST | 63.89 | 56.31 | 44.35 | 55.30 |
| SC | 58.96 | 50.79 | 35.44 | 56.12 |
| Others | 40.90 | 33.80 | 31.20 | 21.94 |
| All | 46.51 | 39.36 | 37.28 | 26.50 |

*Source:* Hann & Dubey (2003).

Social group wise poverty ratio in Orissa during 1983 to 1999-2000 indicates that throughout the periods STs followed by SCs are having the highest incidence of poverty. Reduction in the incidence of poverty in 1993-94 in relation to 1983 has been the lowest among STs. However, the incidence of poverty among all social classes has increased in 1999-00 in comparison to 1993-94. The comparison of the incidence of rural poverty in Orissa in relation to the corresponding figures at All India level indicates that the decline in poverty among all groups at all India level is much faster. In the year 1999-2000, the incidence of rural poverty among the social groups in Orissa is higher than the All India averages among all social groups.

### District-wise and occupational Structure-wise Distribution of Poverty

According to estimates of the Panchayati Raj Department (1992), occupational structure wise classification of the incidence of rural households indicates that maximum concentration of BPL households is reported among marginal farmers (43.05%) followed by agricultural labourers (27.84%), small farmers (16.06%), non-agricultural labourers (8.75%), rural artisans (2.61%) and others (1.25%). BPL families consisting of SFs, MFs and agricultural labourers jointly constitute around 87% of poverty concentration in Orissa (Table 4.6).

**Table 4.6: District-wise and Occupational Structure-wise BPL Families in Orissa**

| | | *Percentage share of BPL families* | | | | | |
|---|---|---|---|---|---|---|---|
| *Sl. No.* | *State/ District* | *SF* | *MF* | *Agricultural* | *Non-Ag. labourers* | *Rural artisans* | *Others* |
| 1 | Sambalpur | 20.68 | 40.40 | 30.46 | 5.91 | 2.55 | 0 |
| 2 | Sundargarh | 31.52 | 44.46 | 10.39 | 12.53 | 1.10 | 0 |
| 3 | Kendujhar | 17.58 | 47.82 | 26.80 | 5.76 | 1.78 | 0 |
| 4 | Mayurbhanj | 18.46 | 51.14 | 21.45 | 4.95 | 1.97 | 2.03 |
| 5 | Balasore | 11.52 | 42.79 | 40.75 | 3.29 | 0.51 | 1.54 |
| 6 | Cuttack | 14.57 | 44.13 | 35.29 | 0 | 6.01 | 0 |

| | | | | | | | |
|---|---|---|---|---|---|---|---|
| 7 | Dhenkanal | 13.67 | 50.75 | 26.47 | 6.37 | 2.24 | 0.47 |
| 8 | Phulbani | 18.50 | 42.48 | 14.89 | 14.50 | 6.83 | 2.79 |
| 9 | Bolangir | 22.16 | 42.88 | 14.89 | 14.50 | 6.83 | 2.79 |
| 10 | Kalahandi | 18.74 | 36.27 | 30.59 | 10.17 | 3.03 | 1.19 |
| 11 | Koraput | 20.56 | 33.31 | 22.60 | 17.48 | 1.87 | 4.18 |
| 12 | Ganjam | 8.75 | 43.51 | 27.35 | 17.37 | 1.80 | 1.22 |
| 13 | Puri | 8.20 | 49.70 | 28.91 | 11.49 | 1.66 | 0 |
| 14 | Orissa | 16.06 | 43.05 | 27.84 | 8.75 | 2.61 | 1.25 |

*Source:* Panchayatiraj Deptt. (1992), Socio-Economic Survey of Rural Household, Panchayatiraj Department, Govt. of Orissa.

## Rural Poverty Trend in Orissa

The long-term trend in the incidence, depth and severity of poverty in rural Orissa is presented in Table 3.7, which reveals that the trend of head count index, poverty gap index and squared poverty gap index is fluctuating over the years during 1957-58 to 1999-2000. Head count index was the highest at 79 percent in 1961-62. It is also observed that the trend of head count index is declining at a faster rate till 1980s and then decreased at a slower rate till 1999-2000. But, the overall linear trend of head count ratio in the state indicates that it is decreasing at a constant rate of 1.03 per annum ('t'=-4.73, F=22.42, R2=0.50). Similar is the case with poverty gap ratio and squared poverty gap ratio. Poverty gap ratio has been decreasing at a constant rate of 0.50 (t= -4.11, F=16.93, R2=0.43) whereas the squared poverty gap index has been decreasing at a significant constant rate of 0.27 ('t'=-4.11, F=16.96, R2=0.43).

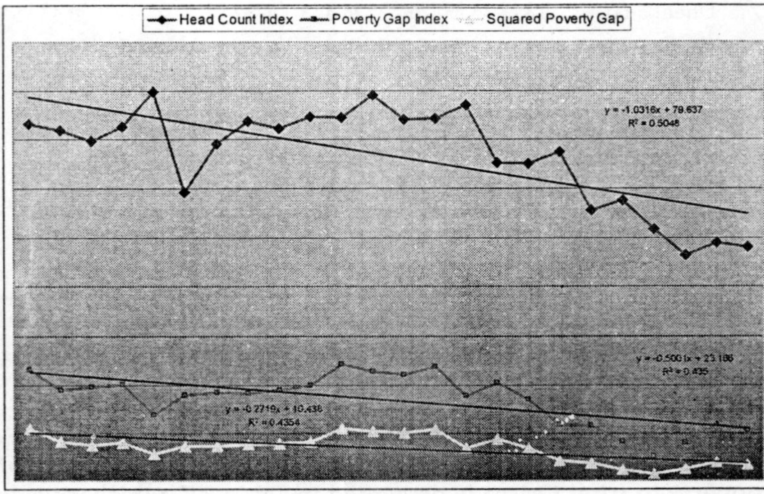


**Fig. 4.2 Rural Poverty Trend in Orissa**

**Table 4.7: Rural Poverty Trends in Orissa**

| *Sl. No.* | *NSSO Survey Period* | *Head Count Index* | *Poverty Gap Index* | *Squared Poverty Gap* |
|---|---|---|---|---|
| 1 | 1957-58 | 73.18 | 23.180 | 11.129 |
| 2 | 1958-59 | 71.88 | 18.967 | 8.474 |
| 3 | 1959-60 | 69.65 | 19.494 | 7.723 |
| 4 | 1960-61 | 72.61 | 20.129 | 8.287 |
| 5 | 1961-62 | 79.84 | 13.909 | 5.912 |
| 6 | 1963-64 | 59.35 | 17.954 | 7.468 |
| 7 | 1964-65 | 69.18 | 18.528 | 7.548 |
| 8 | 1965-66 | 73.74 | 18.280 | 7.806 |
| 9 | 1966-67 | 72.31 | 19.001 | 7.963 |
| 10 | 1967-68 | 74.70 | 19.980 | 8.449 |
| 11 | 1968-69 | 74.43 | 24.308 | 11.070 |
| 12 | 1969-70 | 79.03 | 22.902 | 10.637 |
| 13 | 1970-71 | 74.12 | 22.173 | 10.162 |
| 14 | 1972-73 | 74.20 | 23.693 | 10.952 |
| 15 | 1973-74 | 77.05 | 17.662 | 7.108 |
| 16 | 1977-78 | 65.28 | 20.443 | 8.955 |
| 17 | 1983-84 | 65.21 | 16.962 | 7.126 |
| 18 | 1986-87 | 67.53 | 11.950 | 4.462 |
| 19 | 1987-88 | 55.58 | 11.699 | 3.840 |

| | | | | |
|---|---|---|---|---|
| 20 | 1989-90 | 57.64 | 8.454 | 2.403 |
| 21 | 1990-91 | 51.79 | 5.376 | 1.532 |
| 22 | 1992-93 | 46.39 | 8.195 | 2.530 |
| 23 | 1993-94 | 49.00 | 11.93 | 3.96 |
| 24 | 1999-00 | 48.12 | 10.77 | 3.45 |

*Source:* The World Bank (1997), India: Achievements and Challenges in Reducing Poverty, Washington DC.

## Per Capita Income of Orissa vis-à-vis India

Per capita income is increasingly accepted as a good indicator to examine the percolation of economic growth upon the individuals and it has also strong bearing for assessing income poverty. It is revealed from Table 4.8 that while per capita income at current process for Orissa increased by more than 6 times during the period 1980-81 to 2000-01, the all India per Capita income increased by 9 times. The ratio of per capita income of Orissa to all India per capita income was 0.777 in 1980-81, which declined to 0.518 in 2000-01. The similar trend is noticed in respect of per capita income at constant (1993-94) prices where this ratio has declined from 0.763 in 1980-81 to 0.506 in 2000-01. This clearly indicates that the divergence between per capita income of Orissa and all India is becoming wider day-by-day (Pradhan 2005).

**Table 4.8: Per Capita Income of Orissa in Relation to India at Constant and Current Prices**

| *Year* | *Per capita income at 1993-94* | | | *Per capita income at current price* | | |
|---|---|---|---|---|---|---|
| | *Orissa (NSDP)* | *All India* | *Orissa/ All India* | *Orissa (NSDP)* | *All India* | *Orissa/ All India* |
| 1980-81 | 4085 | 5352 | 0.763 | 1352 | 1741 | 0.777 |
| 1981-82 | 4010 | 5555 | 0.722 | 1485 | 1985 | 0.748 |
| 1982-83 | 3703 | 5555 | 0.667 | 1544 | 2143 | 0.720 |
| 1983-84 | 4374 | 5854 | 0.747 | 1957 | 2464 | 0.794 |
| 1984-85 | 4091 | 5956 | 0.687 | 1899 | 2690 | 0.706 |
| 1985-86 | 4483 | 6082 | 0.737 | 2238 | 2932 | 0.763 |
| 1986-87 | 4464 | 6189 | 0.721 | 2382 | 3191 | 0.747 |
| 1987-88 | 4244 | 6260 | 0.678 | 2375 | 3546 | 0.670 |

| | | | | | | |
|---|---|---|---|---|---|---|
| 1988-89 | 5046 | 6777 | 0.745 | 2954 | 4153 | 0.711 |
| 1989-90 | 5282 | 7087 | 0.745 | 3311 | 4693 | 0.706 |
| 1990-91 | 4300 | 7321 | 0.587 | 3166 | 5365 | 0.590 |
| 1991-92 | 4757 | 7212 | 0.660 | 4020 | 6012 | 0.669 |
| 1992-93 | 4589 | 7433 | 0.617 | 4233 | 6732 | 0.629 |
| 1993-94 | 4797 | 7690 | 0.624 | 4797 | 7690 | 0.624 |
| 1994-95 | 4913 | 8070 | 0.609 | 5638 | 8857 | 0.637 |
| 1995-96 | 5050 | 8489 | 0.596 | 6806 | 10149 | 0.671 |
| 1996-97 | 4652 | 9007 | 0.516 | 6401 | 11564 | 0.554 |
| 1997-98 | 5272 | 9242 | 0.570 | 7831 | 12707 | 0.616 |
| 1998-99 | 5165 | 9647 | 0.535 | 8324 | 14395 | 0.578 |
| 1999-00 | 5265 | 10067 | 0.523 | 8733 | 15562 | 0.561 |
| 2000-01 | 5187 | 10254 | 0.506 | 8547 | 16487 | 0.518 |

*Source:* Pradhan (2005).

## Food Insecurity in Orissa

Due to poor entitlement because of high incidence of poverty, inadequate employment opportunities in lean seasons, and poor economic access to public distribution of subsidized food grains, Orissa has been put in the category of severely food insecure regions. Accesses to food among majority of its population are reported low (Food Insecurity Atlas 2003). Severe food insecurity in Orissa is primarily due to the presence of a vulnerable rural population with poor livelihood access or livelihood susceptible to natural disasters. Lack of safe drinking water, proper health infrastructure, poor rural infrastructure, and low female literacy are the special features of the food insecure State of Orissa (Govt. of Orissa 2004).

In this section, an attempt has been made to examine the food security situation in Orissa in the light of all the existing approaches to define food security. The prominent approaches as already discussed in the previous chapter include FAO Approach (per capita availability of food grains), Poverty Line Approach (calorie shortfall class), WHO Approach (Anthropometric Analysis) and Clinical Malnutrition Approach (outcome symptom assessment among children and pregnant women). All these approaches are attempted to arrive at the malnutrition situation in Orissa.

The situation of 'food security in Orissa' in the light of all these existing approaches is examined as follows:

### FAO Approach

Following the FAO approach food security is viewed according to the available food supply using certain distributional presumptions. For examining food security in Orissa, as per this approach, per capita per day availability of food grains is considered a reasonable indicator. Per capita per day availability of food grains is calculated by dividing annual food supply in Orissa with three sixty five times of its population figure. Annual food supply is arrived at by adding the total food grain production (all serials and all pulses) with the allotment of food grains received from the Government of India during the period under study. Per capita per day availability of food grains (PCPDAFG) is shown in table 4.9.

**Table 4.9: Year Wise Per Capita per day Availability of Food Grains in Orissa**

| *Years* | *Food grain production in (lakh MT)* | *Allotment of Food Grains from Government on India* | | | *Food Supply (in lakh MT* | *Population size (in 000)* | *PCPDAFG (in Kg.)* |
|---|---|---|---|---|---|---|---|
| | | *Rice* | *Wheat* | *Rice+ Wheat* | | | |
| 1996-97 | 48.1 | 10.52 | 4.51 | 14.53 | 62.63 | 3166 | 0.54 |
| 1997-98 | 66.1 | 5.95 | 2.19 | 8.14 | 74.24 | 3166 | 0.64 |
| 1998-99 | 57.9 | 6.57 | 4.35 | 10.92 | 68.82 | 3166 | 0.59 |
| 1999-00 | 90.7 | 11.16 | 3.70 | 14.86 | 105.56 | 3166 | 0.91 |
| 2000-01 | 90.8 | 9.95 | 0.90 | 10.85 | 101.65 | 3670 | 0.75 |
| 2001-02 | 90.9 | 9.97 | 3.0 | 12.7 | 103.60 | 3670 | 0.77 |
| 2002-03 | 91.7 | 27.20 | 3.60 | 30.80 | 122.50 | 3670 | 0.91 |

*Source:* Compiled from different rounds of Economic Survey, Govt. of Orissa.

From this table it is evident that per capita per day availability of food grains is constantly increasing due to increased food production and allotments of food grains received from Government of India. Of course, increased availability of food grains is not reflected in household consumption level because the incidence of poverty in the state stands very high.

Further examination of PCPDAFG in Orissa in comparison to the corresponding figures at all India level reveals that PCPDAFG in Orissa during the period 1996-97 to 2002-03 is higher which is shown in table 4.10. As per this table it is inferred that even though there is better availability of food grains in Orissa, large scale poverty and food insecurity in Orissa are due to the existing bottlenecks in the distribution of food grains and lack of purchasing power of the poor people. This situation is really paradoxical.

**Table 4.10: Comparative Performance of Orissa in PCPDAFG with India**

| *Years* | *PCPDAFG in Orissa** (in Kg.)* | *PCPDAFG in India*** (in K.g.)* |
|---|---|---|
| 1996-97 | 0.54 | 0.47 |
| 1997-98 | 0.64 | 0.50 |
| 1998-99 | 0.59 | 0.44 |
| 1999-00 | 0.91 | 0.46 |
| 2000-01 | 0.75 | 0.45 |
| 2001-02 | 0.77 | 0.41 |
| 2002-03 | 0.91 | 0.49 |

*Source:* *. Compiled from different rounds of Economic survey, Govt. of Orissa.

**. Ministry of Finance, Govt. of India, Economic Survey 2004-05.

## Poverty Line Approach

All the food poverty measurement techniques in general and poverty measurement techniques in particular, except cut off income as stipulated by Panchayatiraj Deptt (people below Rs. 11,000 is identified as BPL) rely on basic energy requirement/basic nutritional requirement at 2400 Kcal per capita per day in rural areas and 2100 Kcal in urban areas. This is the cut off line for calorie poverty. Persons not satisfying this calorie norm are food insecure. However, absolute hunger line in rural areas is fixed at 1800 Kcal (per capita/day). Households fall below this thresh hold calorie are said to be hunger-affected households. The higher incidence of poverty in Orissa is responsible for higher food insecurity and hunger also. In the backward regions and tribal areas, the incidence of poverty is even more than 80 per cent (Pradhan 2003; Sahu 1997; Panda, Panda and Sarangi 2005)

## WHO Approach

WHO approach with the use of anthropometric indicators, measures prevalence of malnutrition in any socio-economic set up. On the basis of anthropometric measures WHO chalks out the extent of malnutrition across the countries, popularly it is viewed as WHO approach. This measure is able to detect malnutrition among any group of people. However, it is best suited to measure malnutrition among children and women. Planning and Co-ordination Department, Govt. of Orissa (2004) views the nutritional status of women and children is a robust indicator of social well-being as they are the most vulnerable sections of the society from the point of view of nutritional stress.

The prevalence of malnutrition among boys, girls and all children (1-5 years) during 1975-79 and 1988-90 is presented in Table 4.11.

**Table 4.11: Percent Distribution of Children (1-5 years) According to Nutritional Grades in Orissa**

*(in percentage)*

| *Children* | *Period* | *Normal* | *Mild* | *Moderate* | *Severe* |
|---|---|---|---|---|---|
| Boys (1-5 years) | 1975-79 | 7.3 | 35.4 | 43.0 | 14.3 |
| | 1988-90 | 7.3 | 35.8 | 46.7 | 10.0 |
| Girls (1-5 years) | 1975-79 | 7.8 | 36.6 | 40.1 | 15.5 |
| | 1988-90 | 8.9 | 33.3 | 46.2 | 11.5 |
| All children (1-5 years) | 1975-79 | 7.5 | 35.9 | 41.7 | 14.9 |
| | 1988-90 | 8.1 | 34.6 | 46.6 | 10.7 |

*Source:* NNMB Repeat Survey (1991).

In Orissa, incidence of under nutrition among children in the age group of 0-5 years is very much disgusting. The proportionate share of undernourished children is reported to be more than 90 percent. Over years, this grave situation has remained unchanged. Again, the prevalence of moderate and severe malnutrition is much higher than mild nutrition over years. The extent of under nutrition among boys and girls are almost equal. During 1991-92, the prevalence of malnourished children declined to 56.2 from 61.5 in 1975-79 and further declined to 47.7 in 2000-01, which is visible across all NNMB sample states, but not reported in Orissa. Malnutrition in Orissa in 2000-01 is about the same as in early 1970s (Radhakrishna, Rao, Ravi, Reddy 2004). It is inferred that over decades the prevalence of malnutrition among 0-5 years children has remained unaltered as per anthropometric indicators. In this context UNICEF (1995) remarks "The risk of death from several of the most common childhood diseases is doubled for a mildly malnourished child, tripled for a moderately malnourished child and multiplied by more than ten times for a severely malnourished child. Upto 80 percent of all children who die of causes related to malnutrition are only mildly and moderately affected."

The Body Mass Index (BMI), which is worked out to assess the nutritional status of population by relating weight with height, is found to be low for women in Orissa. According to National Family Health Survey (1998-99), the average or mean BMI of women in Orissa is 19.2. Chronic energy deficiency is usually indicated by a BMI below 18.5. On this basis, when the nutritional status of women in Orissa is assessed according to the NFHS-2 data, almost 48% of women in the state have a BMI below 18.5, indicating a high prevalence of nutritional deficiency. The survey reveals that nutritional status are particularly serious for younger women, rural women, illiterate women and women for scheduled caste and scheduled tribes (IIPS 1998-99). Similarly around 54 percent of the children below three years of age in Orissa are underweight (weight for age) and 44 percent are stunted (height for age). Among them 21 percent are severely undernourished according to weight for age and

18 percent according to height for age (Planning Commission 2002).

The lower prevalence of the nutrition relevance parameters in Orissa is attributed to higher prevalence of under nutrition among children. A comparative picture of the nutrition relevant parameters for children in Orissa is indicated in Table 4.12 and nutritional status of women is presented in table 4.13

**Table 4.12: Nutrition Relevant Parameters for Children in Orissa in Relation to other States**

| *Sl. No.* | *Nutrition parameters* | *Orissa* | *Andhra Pradesh* | *Kerala* | *All India* |
|---|---|---|---|---|---|
| 1 | Excl bf | 45.7 | 70.5 | 59.2 | 51.0 |
| 2 | Comp feeding | 53.6 | 47.8 | 69.3 | 31.4 |
| 3 | Diarrhoea incidence | 2.5 | 11.7 | 9.2 | 9.9 |
| 4 | ORT Use | 74.7 | 32.2 | 37.8 | 30.5 |
| 5 | Measles | 42.5 | 53.8 | 60.5 | 42.2 |
| 6 | Vit A supp. | NA | NA | NA | 46.0 |
| 7 | IFA Preg | 49.9 | 76.1 | 91.0 | 50.5 |
| 8 | TT Preg | 63.0 | 81.2 | 94.1 | 61.1 |
| 9 | Institutional delivery | 14.2 | 33.0 | 88.4 | 25.5 |

*Source:* National Family Health Survey, India, 1992-93, International Institute for Population Sciences, Mumbai.

NB: Exclusively breast-fed percentage of 0-3 month children who are exclusively breast fed. Complementary feeding - Percentage 6-9 month old children receiving breast milk and solid/mushy foods. Diarrhoea incidence — Percentage of 0-48 month old children reported with diarrhoea in past two weeks. ORT — Percentage of children with diarrhoea in past two weeks give oral rehydration therapy. Measles — Percentage of 12-23-month-old children who had received measles vaccine. Vit A — Percentage of 9-month-old children receiving first dose. IFA Preg. — Percentage of mothers (who gave birth in past four years) receiving iron/folic acid tablets. TT Preg.— Percentage of mothers (who gave birth in past four years) receiving tetanus toxid. Inst.

Delivery — Percentage of mothers (who gave birth in past four years) delivering in private or public institution. Except ORT use and the incidence of measles, in terms of all other nutrition relevant parameters, Orissa's children stand at a disadvantageous position in relation to Kerala, Andhra Pradesh and ali India figures.

## Nutritional Status of Children in Orissa

The nutritional status of children judged on the basis of anthropometric indicators like Weight for age, height for age and weight for height is inferior in Orissa in comparison to Andhra Pradesh, Kerala and all India (Table 4.13).

**Table 4.13: Comparative Nutritional Status of Children in Orissa**

| *Anthropometric Indicators* | *Orissa* | *Andhra Pradesh* | *Kerala* | *All India* |
|---|---|---|---|---|
| Weight for Age | | | | |
| % below -3 SD | 22.7 | 15.6 | 6.1 | 20.6 |
| % below -2 SD | 53.3 | 49.1 | 28.5 | 53.4 |
| Height for Age | | | | |
| % below -3 SD | 25.2 | NA | 9.0 | 28.9 |
| % below -2 SD | 48.2 | NA | 27.4 | 52.0 |
| Weight for Age | | | | |
| % below -3 SD | 3.6 | NA | 1.3 | 3.2 |
| % below -2 SD | 21.3 | NA | 11.6 | 17.5 |

*Source:* NFHS-II (1998-99).

According to WHO approach the children whose weight for age is between 2 and 3 standard deviations of the median reference standard are called Moderate under weight. In comparison to Andhra Pradesh, Kerala and All India figures, the incidence of moderate under-weight in Orissa is found highest at 53.3 per cent. Similarly, the incidence of severe under weight in Orissa is found at 22.7 percent as against Andhra Pradesh (15.6%), Kerala (6.1%) and All India (20.6%). Anthropometric indicator like height-for-age provides the picture of stunting. As per table 4.13, the incidence of moderate stunting (between 2SD -3SD) and severe stunting (below -3SD) in Orissa stands at 48.2 per cent and 25.2 per cent respectively. The corresponding picture in Kerala is much lower. The anthropometric indicator weight-for-height is used to determine short-term or temporary under nutrition. From the above table it is also revealed that the incidence of moderate, temporary under-nutrition in Orissa stands at 21.3 percent and 3.6 percent respectively. The corresponding figures in Kerala and all India is much lower (see Table 4.13).

## Nutritional Status of Women in Orissa

On the basis of anthropometrics indicators as shown in table 4.14 the nutritional status of women in Orissa is found to be lower in comparison to Andhra Pradesh, Kerala and all India figures. The mean height of women in Orissa is lower than that of Andhra Pradesh and Kerala. Percentage of women below 145 cms., called as stunted category is much higher in Orissa in comparison to Kerala. Similarly, the women of Orissa are marginally worse of in comparison to Andhra Pradesh. The mean Body Mass Index (BMI) used as an anthropometric tool to measure under nutrition stands at 19.2 in Orissa. The corresponding figures for Kerala, Andhra Pradesh, and All India are 22.0, 20.3 and 20.3 respectively. Around 39 % of women in Orissa are below the prescribed BMI of 18.5 kg/m2 indicating that the nutritional status of a significant majority of women is poor.

**Table 4.14: Comparative Nutritional Status of Women in Orissa**

| *Sl. No.* | *Nutrition parameters* | *Orissa* | *Andhra Pradesh* | *Kerla* | *All India* |
|---|---|---|---|---|---|
| | Height | | | | |
| 1 | Mean Height (Cm.) | 150.5 | 151.2 | 152.6 | 151.2 |
| 2 | % below 145 cms. | 14.9 | 12.7 | 8.8 | 13.2 |
| | Weight for height | | | | |
| 3 | Mean Body Mass Index | 19.2 | 20.3 | 22.0 | 20.3 |
| 4 | % with BMI below 18.5 kg./m2 | 39.3 | 37.4 | 18.7 | 35.8 |

*Source:* NFHS-II (1998-99).

## Clinical Malnutrition Approach

In addition to food energy intake measures (per capita availability of food grains and poverty line approach) and anthropometric measures, clinical signs are used for the assessment of malnutrition. Several studies have indicated this concept as clinical malnutrition (UNICEF 1995, Rao 1994, Radhakrishna 2004). Clinical evaluation indicated that every fifth child examined showed deficiency sign of some nutrient or other. Signs of protein energy malnutrition and vitamin 'A' and 'B' complex deficiency were the most common disorders (Rao 1994). A comparative picture of prevalence of nutritional deficiency signs in Orissa is presented in table 4.15.

**Table 4.15: Percent Prevalence of Nutritional Deficiency Signs in Orissa in Relation to other States**

| *Sl. No.* | *Nutritional deficiency signs* | *Period of survey* | *Orissa* | *Kerala* | *Andhra Pradesh* | *All India (Pooled)* |
|---|---|---|---|---|---|---|
| 1 | Oedema | 1975-79 | - | - | 0.9 | 0.4 |
| | | 1988-90 | - | - | - | 0.1 |
| 2 | Marasmus | 1975-79 | 0.6 | 0.2 | 2.0 | 1.3 |
| | | 1988-90 | 0.1 | 0.1 | 0.1 | 0.6 |
| 3 | Two or more signs of protein energy malnutrition | 1975-79 | - | 0.2 | 0.9 | 1.2 |
| | | 1988-90 | 0.1 | - | 0.1 | 0.2 |
| 4 | Bitot's spots | 1975-79 | 1.5 | 0.1 | 3.1 | 1.8 |
| | | 1988-90 | 1.1 | 0.5 | 1.0 | 0.7 |
| 5 | Angular Stomatitis | 1975-79 | 5.9 | 1.6 | 7.9 | 5.7 |
| | | 1988-90 | - | - | 9.0 | 5.7 |
| 6 | Vitamin A Deficiency (VAD) | 1975-79 | 76.3 | 91.7 | 79.8 | 80.7 |
| | | 1988-90 | 96.3 | 94.5 | 88.5 | 83.5 |
| Number of Children identified | | 1975-79 | 660 | 1034 | 2361 | 12755 |
| | | 1988-90 | 911 | 2792 | 2394 | 11535 |

*Source:* NNMB Repeat Survey (1991).

Table 4.15 reveals that during 1975-79 to 1988-90 prevalence of nutritional deficiency signs in all the three states has increased in absolute as well as percentage terms. However, the incidence of clinical malnutrition is reported maximum in Andhra Pradesh, but over years, the rate of increase is almost negligible. It is further indicated that all the states including Orissa, nutritional deficiency signs are more concentrated around VAD.

## Rural Employment in Orissa

The issue of rural employment is the key to poverty reduction and improvement in standard of living as the trend, structure and dimension of rural employment considerably influence the nature of social and economic change in a society. Orissa is one of the backward states in India experienced that every section of workforce and most sectors of the economy suffered a shock in terms of employment growth over period. A depressing rural employment scenario is evident with worse suffering on rural females, although here was a marginal decline in labour force and work participation rates in the state. Rural workers constitute about 89 percent of total workers and there was a decline in the share of rural workers in all industry groups during late 1990s. Similarly, rural females accounts about 35 percent of total rural employment has been marginally declining. It may be seen in the Table-3 and 4 during 1999-00 agriculture accommodates about 79 percent of total rural worker, relatively higher proportion of females, followed by manufacturing 9 percent. There is hardly any decline in farm sector employment in rural areas. But a drastic decline in male worker employment in manufacturing sector from 8 percent to 6.23 percent between 1983 and 1999-00 is reported where as the proportion of female workers engaged in manufacturing sector has not only been increased from 9.9 percent to 12.6 percent which is relatively higher than their male counterparts during this period. It seems that there has been shift of rural employment from male workers to female workers in manufacturing sector. Similarly, for rural male, such a trend is visible in the construction and trade sector. It may be noted that increasing participation of rural female in low productive traditional caste based rural manufacturing activity due to lack of productive farm employment could explain this shift (Sahu, 2003). From policy point of view, it needs further detail study to understand this trend vis-à-vis growth of rural non-farm employment and its impact on overall rural economy.

From rural employment front, another important trend in Orissa is the progressive casualisation of rural employment. Sharp decline in self-employment, particularly in terms of cultivators and increasing in agricultural labourers over period in Orissa show the increasing marginalisation of rural jobs and segmented labour market. Under this situation, while rural male workers suffer in terms of rate of employment and mig tion, rural female workers suffer much in terms of productivity, flexibility of choice of jobs and regularity of employment. In sum, quality of rural employment, in the absence of a productive agriculture and sustainable non-farm sector, remain the key policy issue foe backward state like Orissa. Unfortunately the pace of non-farm sector employment has not increased over period. In backward rural areas the growth non-farm sector is largely due to distress factors (Sahu 2003). Rural employment growth has declined for all section of workers, both for males (1.46 to 0.86 percent) and females (2.26 to 31 percent) during 1990s, more sharper for females.

- Sectors reporting higher or increasing employment growth, such as mining, utilities, transport & communication, real estate and financial services, fail to compensate decline in employment growth in the rural areas during 1990s due to the nature and structure and ability to absorb rural people.
- Low and sharp decline in farm sector employment is the major factor for the poor rural employment and development. Within agriculture, sub-sectors like fishing, forestry, livestock and agricultural services experienced negative employment growth during 1990s. However, SDP growth in these sectors has been notable during same period.
- Highly disparate trend in rural employment is evident

during 1990s over 1980s. Benefits of improved employment are not accessible to the rural people due to lack of their capability, skills location and information.

- Pace of rural non-farm employment, though increased but failed to absorb surplus rural labour productively to compensate decline in farm employment.

In sum, rural areas in Orissa as experienced a disadvantage employment situation, particularly in 1990s, with worse effect on female workers. Diversification of rural employment remains at halting pace with hardly any improvement in quality of employment.

## Agrarian Structure and Access to Land

Land is the single most important factor for rural livelihood and rural poverty. Land distribution is highly unequal and access to land by the many poor is not easy under present land system in Orissa. The agrarian structure in the state has not been favorable enough to achieve a fairly high agricultural growth rate across the regions. High inequality in asset holding, lack of irrigation, lack of formal credit, high transaction cost, poor performance of institutions and other factors discourage many small and marginal farmers to invest in productive investment or make them unable to exploit growth-promoting opportunities. Inadequate property right and poor access to land by the weaker section remain major constrain for regional growth. Mohanty (2001) notes that in Orissa the operational holdings belonging to scheduled castes increased slightly, but worsened slightly for scheduled tribes during the 1980s.

Dominance and increase in marginal holdings (82% of holdings and 50% of operated area) in the state shows that the inequality in the distribution of operational land has not been helpful in accelerating agricultural productivity and growth. The per capita availability of cultivated land has drastically declined from 0.39 ha in 1950-51, to 0.14 ha in 2000-2001. The average operated area per holding has declined from 1.47 ha in 1985-86 to 1.34 ha during 1995-96 (Agricultural Census, Orissa 1995-96).

In spite of predominance of small and marginal farmers the land policy in the state, though reduced the operational area held under large holdings, failed to distribute the gains among marginal groups. On the other hand proportion of household operating with no land, but depend mainly on agricultural labour, increased substantially, accounting for one-third of total households. Off late, some landless gained access to land but their total numbers limited to a quarter of all households in the state. During last half century there has been hardly any improvement in access to arable land by the poor, which could have the best way out of poverty. Thus the present land holding system and agrarian structure may contribute to the poor growth and slow poverty reduction and dismal performance of rural areas in the state.

Though the gains to backward groups (SC & ST) in total land are evident at national and the state level, there is hardly any change in the incidence of overall landlessness in Orissa. Interestingly, in early 1990s the share of ST households in total land has increased appreciably higher than their share in total population, yet incidence of landlessness among tribal has increased in the state (see table – 8). As regard to concentration of land it increased in Orissa over period but at least not for ST households. While the proportion of large holding marginally decline and proportion of marginal holding has increased in all groups over period it is more pronounced during 1980s and among backward groups. Under land reforms the major gains have been in the share of medium sized holding. Marginal and small holding, accounts more than half of total operational holdings, experienced no remarkable increase in the share of area. On the other hand though some landless people gained access to land during 1960s but households operating no land have increased substantially during later period. Hence, land policy during last fifty years seems hardly improve the land distribution which become the formidable obstacle to prevent improving access to land by the poor, accelerating rural growth and reduction of poverty in the state.

However, access to land through tenancy remains substantial in backward agriculture like Orissa. In fact, where markets for land, credit, labour, information, insurance and management are missing tenancy play important role in managing productive factors like land, labour and capital. High incidence of tenancy in the state is another important factor that determines the growth of productivity. As per NSS (50th Round 1992), 22% of cultivators were tenant farmers covering 11.3% cultivated area. But the tenancy in the state is more of subsistence type, having poor capacity to invest and no access to formal credit. As a result it does not contribute much to the rate of agricultural productivity of the state. It may be noted that the average area leased in per reporting tenant household was merely 0.38 ha during the 1990s. Sharecropping is the dominant form of tenancy followed by fixed rent. Most of the tenant cultivators have no clear property rights on land and the contracts are short term and oral in nature. In such a situation, there is no incentive for hard work on the tenanted land. A majority of tenants have to depend on the landlord–creditor to arrange working capital requirements. Moreover, the land records are not up-to-date and there is the presence of joint-holdings. As a result, many farmers even if cultivating land for many years, have no clear-cut property rights on the land and hence unable to borrow from the formal credit sector.

Thus, Orissa provides unique picture of tenancy where nature and extent of lease market and terms of tenancy vary across different parts of the state and social groups. Some field-based studies (Sarap 1998, Swain 1999) estimate that about 20 percent of farm households and one-fourth of total operated area are under tenancy in the state. There is widespread land transaction in lease markets and about 80 percent of leasing activity is carried out by small and marginal farmer. In spite of several tenancy legislations, land under tenancy system remains high, especially under share tenancy contract and most of land lease markets operate in oral and concealed manner. Sahu (2004) found some notable trend in land holding and tenancy in Orissa that influence agriculture and rural poverty are :

- Unlike many other states, the proportion of owned self-cultivated holdings declined during 1991-92 in Orissa with a progressive decline in the share of entirely leased-in holdings and mixed holding in the state.

- While there is no remarkable increase in leased and owned holdings the number of possessed holding increased, may be due to increase in encroachment of govt. land and poor land administration resulting in incomplete transfer of ownership rights of holdings under tenants possession.
- The proportion of leased in area to total operated area declined in Orissa during 1970s but no remarkable change thereafter. Unlike in other states, the change in the share of owned or leased holding was marginal while area under these categories remained unchanged during 1980s in Orissa.
- While there was significant decline in proportion of holding and area under share crop tenancy elsewhere, it increased in Orissa during 1981-82 to 1991-92. This indicates the significance of tenancy under uncertain backward agriculture like Orissa, which is different from many other states. However, the proportion of holding and area leasing-in under fixed produce terms declined in Orissa though under fixed money term it increased during 1981-82 to 1991-92, more sharply than national level.
- share tenancy accounts more than half of total area and holding under total tenancy in Orissa which is higher than national level. Within the state, very high rate of share crop tenancy and decline in fixed tenancy, particularly dry/arid areas. This shows greater potential of share tenancy in a backward agriculture to share risk between tenants and landowners.

In sum, glaring inequality in land distribution and land access is evident in the state. Land policy in the state has failed in improving overall situation of marginal groups. Landlessness among backward castes (SC, ST) marginally rises over period which might have deteriorated their socio-economic condition. Above discussion supports the fact that current land base of marginal groups has not been effective in improving their well-being. Existing land practices state that tenancy is a response to missing market, especially for rural labour. Concealing tenancy affects tenants adversely by denying them security of tenure and consequently limiting their access to credit and other assets. However, heterogeneity in tenancy contract in the state seems to confirm the presence of potential for risk-sharing under share cropping contract.

Therefore, effective mechanism to increase access of land to rural poor may be considered at policy level as high incidence tenancy and encroachment are reported in the state. Liberalisation of land lease market may be a well come measure with right balance between long-term ownership right for landowner and assuring tenants of their security of tenure, protection and access to credit. Deregulation of tenancy may encourage large landowner to participate in land lease-out which will enhance land access of poor and increase govt. revenue.

However, the prevailing social and cultural norms may be more important than state legislation for land transactions between similar groups, caste and class as they are relatively non-exploitative. Tenurial security through well defined property rights, even for short period may enable the poor to access institutional credit and thereby improve agricultural productivity. The typical agrarian structure and trends in tenancy in Orissa considerably influence agricultural productivity, adoption of agricultural technology and practices, poverty and livelihood in the rural areas.

## Agricultural Development

High agricultural productivity is crucial for rural development as well as reducing rural urban gap through accelerating growth and extending bulk of the gains to the poor in terms of higher farm yield and higher real wages. In Orissa, the performance of primary sector which dominant in terms of contribution to state domestic product was poor in 1990s than in 1980s. Within the primary sector, agriculture faced major setback particularly in 1990s. This is a serious concern for rural growth and poverty reduction. The poor performance of agriculture sector has been due to a variety of factors originating both at regional and state level. For instance the availability of irrigation facility, adoption of modern inputs in southern and some northern districts of the state are much below even the state average. Further uncertain property rights in land among marginal groups make their access to resource problematic. In such a situation it becomes difficult even for those households having certain land resource to utilize it properly in the absence of complementary resource (credit).

Low agricultural productivity in the state is constrained by several factors — ever declining land-man ratio, increasing marginalization of holdings, poor irrigation network, lack of formal credit, poor adoption of new farm technology and declining capital expenditure in agriculture. Therefore, fostering the conditions for rural economic growth especially in agriculture and rural development is crucial to poverty reduction, in a state like Orissa.

From the aforesaid discussion made in this chapter it is clear that Orissa is a poverty ridden state, where the incidence of rural poverty and consequently malnutrition is significantly noticed. Rural areas in Orissa experience a disadvantageous employment situation, particularly in 1990s, with worse effect on female workers. Diversification of rural employment remains at halting pace with hardly any improvement in quality of employment. Ever declining land-man ratio, increasing marginalization of holdings, poor irrigation network, lack of formal credit, poor adoption of new farm technology and declining capital expenditure in agriculture are some of the important reasons for agricultural backwardness of the state. Therefore, fostering the conditions for rural economic growth especially in agriculture and rural development is crucial to poverty reduction, in a state like Orissa.

# 5

# Profile of the Bureaucrats in Orissa

For a better understanding of the bureaucrats, It is necessary to understand their socio-economic background. The study of the socio-economic background of the bureaucrats is of special significance in a stratified society like orissa where the forces of caste and kinship influence the social life and where acute disparities exist in the standard of living and sub-culture among various groups and regions. The existence of inequality between the elite and the general masses and the slow process of occupational mobility emphasize the need for a study of the socio-economic background of the bureaucrats. In fact the study of socio-economic background of the bureaucrats gives rise to an important question: How far is the bureaucracy representative of a society? This representative character of bureaucracy is of great importance to a democratic country because it helps in the articulation of values and interests of different classes and strata which are brought to bear upon the decisions taken and policies formulated by it (V Subramanian(1971), *Social Background of India's Administrators,* Publication division, Ministry of Information and Broadcasting, Government of India, New Delhi). Norton E. Long(1952) goes so far as to say that bureaucracy is a better sample of the masses than the democratic legislature. He points out that important interests, which are misrepresented or unrepresented in the legislature, receive effective representation through administrative channels. It can serve democratic process from being bogged down and can come to be recognized as 'the great fourth branch of the government'. It is more so in a society like India which is divided into caste, religious groups and linguistic and regional sub-divisions. The divisions of caste being based on the accident of birth are more rigid than the class divisions because the former are ascriptive. One's status in them cannot be achieved and concequentlu there is less social mobility. This division of society makes it desirable that the country's bureaucracy should represent different castes and religious groups and also the different regions, so that, all the sections of the society with diverse interests can find representation in the formulation and implementation of policies. In the absence of this, there is the probability of sectional and parochial sympathies and even loyalties of the bureaucrats influencing their work leading to a neglect of the interests of the unrepresented sections. As Kelsall has shown, the middle class origin of the British Civil Service is a factor responsible for its being out of touch with the problems of the working class (Subramaniam, 1967).

The class origin of the bureaucrats has an important bearing upon the functioning of bureaucracy, because it is generally recognized that an administrator brings with him certain attitudes and values which he develops before joining the administration, and the development of the attitudes and values is influenced by the familial, social and other environmental conditions in which the administrator is brought up. The attitudes and values which the bureaucrats develop before joining the bureaucracy greatly influence his future course of action. Although it is a fact that the bureaucratic cultural pattern in which he works may either modify or reinforce his attitudes and values that he develops prior to joining the bureaucracy. Related to the representative ness of the higher bureaucracy, a question may be raised here as to how far does the background of the background reveal the regional, linguistic, social and cultural heterogeneity. The answer to this question may help us in understanding the contribution of higher bureaucracy to the preservation of the unity of the nation as well as to the developmental process (Singh, 1974). In the remaining section of this chapter, an attempt is made to study the age group, sex, Provincial background, religion, nature of schooling/educational qualification, occupation and income.

## 5.1 Age Group

Age group of the bureaucrats is an important factor in their functionings and value orientations. At a young age, one is considered to be harder working, energetic and full of initiative and the spirit of enterprise then in one's old age. Later years of one's career are marked by maturity, thought fullness and cautious approach. Man acquires experience with his age which helps him in taking decisions and formulating policies in the light of his past experience. And the experience which one gains with one's age also shapes and reshapes one's values which has an impact upon one self and the organization or unit of the system of which one is part. The principle of early age recruitment was advocated by Lord Macaulay which has been a feature of Civil Service Recruitment in India since the days of the East India Company. At present the minimum age limit for competitive examinations in state and all- India services is twenty one years and the maximum age limit is twenty eight years in the case of Central and all India Services. The maximum age limit in case of state services varies from state to state. In the case of Orissa, the maximum age limit is thirty two years. The pattern of age structure of the bureaucrats on the basis of different categories of positions enjoyed by them in Orissa is furnished in table 1.

**Table 1: Age Group-wise Distribution of IAS Officers in Orissa**

| *Sl No* | *Age Group (in Years)* | *No of IAS offices* | *%* |
|---|---|---|---|
| 1 | 25-35 | 25 | 14.79 |
| 2 | 35-45 | 46 | 27.21 |
| 3 | 45-55 | 44 | 26.03 |
| 4 | >55 | 54 | 31.95 |
| | Total | 169 | 100.00 |

## Sex

Sex is an important factor in the study of bureaucracy in India where the position of women is comparatively low. There is also a popular assumption that women are both physically and intellectually weak in comparison with men and the proper sphere of women is the management is the management of household affairs. At the beginning of this century, there were very few women who were in public service. But with the passage of time, this barrier has been broken and especially after independence more and more women have been competing for joining into the public service. At present, an increasing number of women candidates are joining the All-India and Central Services. In this background, it is of special interest to categorise the Orissa level bureaucrats on the basis of their sex. The distribution of the bureaucrats on the basis of sex is shown in the following table-2.

**Table 2: Distribution of IAS Officers on the Basis of Sex**

| *Sl No* | *Age Group (in Years)* | *No of IAS offices* | *%* |
|---|---|---|---|
| 1 | Male | 151 | 89.34 |
| 2 | Female | 18 | 10.66 |
| | Total | 169 | 100.00 |

## Provincial Background

Provincial background is an important dimension in the study of bureaucracy in a country like India where great diversities exist within the states. This sometimes give rise to communalism, casteism, and sub regionalism. But such type of antagonistic feelings have never taken place in Orissa. Rather outsiders have received overwhelming support by the people of Orissa. The provincial background of the bureaucrats in Orissa is shown in Table-3. As the study considers both IAS and OAS cadre administrators as bureaucrats, but here purposefully only IAS cadre bureaucrats is considered as there is very little provincial difference among the OAS type of bureaucrats. The proportionate share of different provinces among the bureaucrats is shown in Table-3. In this table further bifurcation has been made for technical and non technical type of bureaucracy.

**Table 3: State Cadre-wise Distribution of IAS Officers**

| *Sl No* | *State Cadres* | *No of IAS offices* | *Percentage* |
|---|---|---|---|
| 1 | Orissa | 78 | 46.15 |
| 2 | Delhi | 10 | 5.91 |
| 3 | UP | 15 | 8.90 |
| 4 | Bihar | 13 | 7.69 |
| 5 | Tamilnadu | 16 | 9.46 |
| 6 | West Bengal | 6 | 3.55 |
| 7 | Punjab | 5 | 2.95 |
| 8 | Maharashtra | 4 | 2.36 |
| 9 | Kerala | 2 | 1.18 |
| 10 | Rajasthan | 10 | 5.91 |
| 11 | Karnataka | 3 | 1.77 |
| 12 | Andhra Pradesh | 5 | 2.95 |
| 13 | Himachal Pradesh | 1 | 0.59 |
| 14 | Chandigarh | 1 | 0.59 |
| 15 | Madhya Pradesh | 2 | 1.18 |
| 16 | Assam | 1 | 0.59 |
| 17 | Nagaland | 1 | 0.59 |
| 18 | Haryana | 1 | 0.59 |
| 19 | Jammu/Kashmir | 1 | 0.59 |
| | TOTAL | 169 | 100.00 |

## Rural-Urban Background

The underlying importance of the study of the rural-urban background of the bureaucrats is that it influences their norms, values and behaviour patterns which have been an important bearing on their functioning. As the facilities available in urban areas are different from those of the rural areas, the process of socialization also tends to be different in rural-urban settings. Persons living in urban areas are exposed to scientific and industrial development. Thus rural-urban background not only affects the functioning of bureaucracy but also the value orientation of the bureaucrats which influences the strategy of development and modernization. It is reported that more than 90 percent of the IAS officers are hailed from urban background.

## Religious Background

India is committed to the ideals of secularism and equality of opportunity for government employment irrespective of religion, caste or region. This has been well proved by electing persons from the minority community to the highest office under the Indian Constitution. Although religion is not a qualification for entering into public service, in order to be representative, public service must represent people of different religious communities as it helps in the articulation of values and interests of the different classes. Demands are not infrequent for the reservation of seats in the public services for those minority communities which are not well represented. It will, therefore be useful to examine whether different religious groups are represented in the bureaucracy in Orissa.

## Social Background

The Constitution of India has provided special safeguards to the scheduled castes and scheduled tribes in Government jobs and educational institutes in order to improve their lot. But this policy has given a new lease of life to caste divisions in India. The Policy of providing special benefits to persons on the basis of caste and tribe has caused dissatisfaction in the minds of the people and is responsible for creating social antagonism and tensions. The policy of special benefits was found to be one of the causes of increased atrocities on SC and ST category of people during different period of time during the post independent India. It is to note that during early 1990s, at the outbreak of Mandal Commission Report for guaranteeing reservation to the OBC category of people there was massive violence and agitation throughout India. In this background it is felt imperative to study the social background of the IAS officers working in Orissa. Educational Background.

Education is another important dimension for understanding the socio-economic background of the bureaucrats. It is more so in a country like India where educational facilities are unevenly distributed. Here we will study the nature of schooling and educational background of the bureaucrats.

## Nature of Schooling

The bureaucracy in India is by and large composed of the intellectually best endowed graduates. For entering into bureaucratic services, the candidates have to face a tough competition and need a high level of intellectual ability. The development of intellectual ability depends to a great extent, upon the nature of education at the school and college level. "It is at the school stage that the foundation of the super structure of the university structure is laid down. For, what an individual learns in schools like what he learns at home from the members of his family, weighs heavily in determining which relatively full time, functionally significant social roles he will be able to fulfil."

But there is difficulty in classifying the schools. The common classification of public and private schools seems to be unsatisfactory because what is public in one context may be private in different context. Of course there is no full proof classification as every classification has some shortcomings. However we would classify the schools here on the basis of medium of instruction i.e. English medium schools and Vernacular schools.

Though the quality of education does not depend upon the medium through which knowledge is imparted, it is generally believed that some personal traits like smartness, discipline, fluent speaking, social graces, proficiency in sports and games etc are developed more in the English medium schools than in the vernacular schools. And this is the reason why the well to do families are interested to send their children in English–medium schools.

## Educational Qualification

The study of educational qualifications also helps us in understanding the socio-economic background of the bureaucrats. The minimum educational qualifications prescribed for the IAS and Allied Services and the State

Services is the ordinary first degree of an university. But recent studies suggest that the recruitment system for bureaucracy favours those candidates whose qualifications are higher than the minimum qualifications formally prescribed. The educational qualification of the Orissa level bureaucrats is shown in the following table-4.

**Table 4: Educational Background of IAS Officers**

| *Sl No* | *Level of Education* | *No of IAS offices* | *%* |
|---|---|---|---|
| 1 | BA | 15 | 8.87 |
| 2 | BSc | 2 | 1.18 |
| 3 | B Com | 1 | 0.59 |
| 4 | MA | 68 | 40.23 |
| 5 | MSc | 24 | 14.20 |
| 6 | MBA | 6 | 3.55 |
| 7 | Engineering | 36 | 21.30 |
| 8 | MBBS | 7 | 4.14 |
| 9 | Above Master Degree | 10 | 5.91 |
| | TOTAL | 169 | 100.00 |

## Hierarchy of Administration

The state administration is hierarchical. At the apex is the governor-the symbolic head. The council of ministers with the chief minister at its head administer the state and implement developmental programmes through administrative departments at the secreteriat and directorate levels, where IAS, OAS, OFS and personnels of secreterial service work together. The chief secretary coordinates the works of all the departments. At the district level, the district collector plays the key role and he is the coordinator and implementor of development administration. At the Sub division level SDO (Sub Collector) has the key role of administration. At the block level, Block Development Officer (BDO) takes the responsibility of executing and monitoring the programmes. With the introduction of Panchayatiraj a structure has emerged at the district level where the collector's association with the emergent system and the role assigned to him varied from state to state (Goswamy 1955). The role of collector in development administration does not find a 'clear' and 'precise' definition. Except in the fields of revenue, law and order and natural calamities, his role as a coordinator seems to be nebulous (Dayal et al 1976). In Orissa, the collector very often faces the problems of departmental verification while seeking horizontal coordination at the district level as the functionaries of all technical departments, who are under him deal directly with their respective departmental heads at the state head quarters. Today's collectors have been exposed to so many stresses and strains that he has become a busy man having no time and energy to get deep into any matter and pursue things to their logical conclusion. Similarly the collector is not able to effectively supervise municipal administration. The relationship between the Collector and local bodies seems to be poor (Anand 1988). In Orissa the collector and District Magistrate of a district is simultaneously the head of criminal, Revenue and Development administration in the district. Being the head of the district the collector has to coordinate Department of Agriculture, Fishery, Co-operation, Community Development, Social Welfare Department, Transport, Mining etc.

Thus, it can be seen that in Orissa there is no bifurcation between regulatory and development administration. As a result, the responsibilities of the collector are enormous whereas powers at his command are few (Tripathy, 1988).

In Orissa, another aspect of state administration which accounts for slow implementation of programmes relates to lack of rapport between the politicians and the bureaucrats. There is "Subterranean Misunderstanding" between them. The politician tends to dictate and boss over the bureaucracy and the latter surreptitiously (Das and Pradhan 1988). Both the politicians and the bureaucrats in Orissa must understand and cooperate with each other for the development of the state.

In the fitness of this chapter, the socio-economic background of the bureaucrats reveals that bureaucracy in Orissa far from being representative in character, is a monopoly of the urban middle class elites. After five decades of independence, there is very little change in the nature of the bureaucracy. Still bureaucracy is virtually closed to men and women from rural background. The restrictive nature of bureaucracy in terms of socio-economic background is a problem for the effective implementation of the development programmes because development interventions are mainly taking place in rural areas. As per the analysis of the hierarchy of administration, it is found that state administration which accounts for slow implementation of programmes relates to lack of rapport between the politicians and the bureaucrats. There is "Subterranean Misunderstanding" between them. The politician tends to dictate and boss over the bureaucracy and the latter surreptitiously (Das and Pradhan 1988). Both the politicians and the bureaucrats in Orissa must understand and cooperate with each other for the development of the state.

# 6

# Role of Bureaucracy in Economic Development: A Case Study of Watershed Programme and Joint Forest Management Programme

In recent years particularly since early 1990s, the government of India has been trying to shift its traditional role from a mere provider to a facilitator for the rural socio-economic transformation. The process involves people's participation not only in cost sharing but also in planning, design, implementation, surveillance and operational maintenance of the schemes in collaboration with various other government sectors. On the recommendations of the Hanumantha Rao Committee, the two Area Development Programmes and the development of wastelands are to be taken up through community participation following a watershed approach under common guidelines with effect from 1st April, 1995. A watershed is a geo-hydrological unit, which drains into a common point. It is a project based, ridge to valley approach for *in-situ* soil and water conservation, afforestation etc. and it includes:

The Department of Land Resources in the Ministry

of Rural Development is administering three area-based watershed programmes for development of wastelands/degraded lands namely Drought Prone Areas Programmes (DPAP), Desert Development Programme (DDP) and Integrated Wastelands Development Programme (IWDP) with a view to achieve allround socio economic development in the rural and tribal areas. The DPAP was launched in 1973-74 to tackle the special problems faced by those areas that are constantly afflicted by drought conditions. Presently, 972 blocks of 195 districts in 16 States are covered under the Programme. DDP was launched in 1977-78 to mitigate the adverse effects of desertification. Presently, 235 blocks of 40 districts in 7 States are covered under the Programme. IWDP has been under implementation since 1989-90. The programme is being implemented in 216 districts of the country. DoLR is also initiating measures aimed at enabling a greater role for Panchayati Raj Institutions (PRIs), Self-help groups (SHGs) and user-groups particularly the landless belonging to the Scheduled Castes (SCs) & Scheduled Tribes (STs) and other backward classes, in watershed programmes.

The projects under the IWDP are generally sanctioned in areas that are not covered under DDP or DPAP. Since 1 April 1995, these three programmes are being implemented on the basis of Common Guidelines for Watershed Development In case of IWDP, the cost sharing between the Centre and State Governments is in the ratio of 11:1. Funds are released in seven installments, six installments at the rate of 15 per cent and the last installment at the rate of 10 per cent. Projects are implemented by District Rural Development Agencies/Zilla Parishads (DRDAs/ZPs) through Project Implementing Agencies (PIAs). PIAs could be a Line Department (of the State Government), Panchayati Raj Institutions or a reputed NGO. One PIA normally handles 10-12 watershed projects covering an area of about 5000-6000 hectares. The PIA is required to maintain a technical team of 4 experts called Watershed Development Team (WDT) and individual projects (500 hectares) are planned and executed by the local people living in the watershed area called the Watershed Association (WA) through an elected body called Watershed Committee (WC). The Programme is expected to promote the generation of employment in the rural areas besides enhancing people's participation at all stages in the development of wastelands—leading to sustainable development and equitable sharing of the benefits. It is a 100 percent Central sector scheme. Project Director of the DRDA and Collector of the concerned district and are the authorities to continuously monitor the programme. Collector is the chairman of the District level Watershed Committee. The role of the collector is to look after the following issues.

- Collection of balance beneficiary's contribution and procurement of materials will be done prior to the actual implementation of the scheme.
- Supervision will be done by Village Watershed Committee (VWC) and District Watershed Committee(DWC).
- Completion, commissioning and handing-over of completed scheme to the villagers/VSC for its continued Operation and Maintenance.
- Monitoring, Evaluation & Surveillance of the projects.
- A continuous process of monitoring & evaluation, review, mid-course correction (if any required) will be carried out by DWC, State Government.
- Concurrent activities during and post project implementation.

Similarly, as per the provisions of National Forest Policy 1988, the Government of India, vide letter NO.6.21/89-PP dated 1st June, 1990, outlined and conveyed to State Governments a framework for creating massive people's movement through involvement of village committees for the protection, regeneration and development of degraded forest lands. This gave impetus to the participation of stakeholders in the management of degraded forests situated in the vicinity of villages. The joint forest management programme in the country is structured on the broad framework provided by the guidelines issued by the Ministry. So far, during the last ten years, 27 State Governments have adopted resolutions for implementing the JFM programme in their respective states. As on 15.8.2001, 14254845.95 ha of forests lands are being managed under JFM programme through 62890 committees. The JFM programme in the country is reviewed by Government of India from time to time in consultation with State Governments, NGO's and other stakeholders in view of its socio economic importance. While technical consideration in Indian Forestry has remained unchanged over the past century, the objectives of forest management have undergone many changes over the same period. These changes are distinct with respect to the JFM programme, which envisages the rehabilitation of degraded forests through natural regeneration and improving productivity of forest products, particularly NTFPs, to meet village communities' requirements. Specific aspects like regeneration of degraded lands, nursery management, NTFP management, fodder management, fuelwood management, fire management and the importance of protection as an important technique to regenerate the forest areas, have come to fore. It is essential that capacity building of villagers be carried out at the earliest on different aspects of JFM including concept, duties and responsibilities, microplanning, process documentation, monitoring, plantation, forest operations, and nursery techniques. Biodiversity conservation should be given due importance in training programmes. NGOs could be involved in undertaking these training programmes. Frequent impact assessment and monitoring of JFM activities including forestry operations by the communities would help ease the load on FD staff. For monitoring forest changes, in addition to permanent plots and baseline surveys, experimental plots should also be laid in the forest areas by the FD and VFCs. The 1990 guidelines have paved the way for JFM across the country and 22 states have issued enabling orders till date. Different State Governments have issued orders and modified the same progressively to incorporate variations and major concerns that have arisen during the course of JFM implementation in their respective states. States have also issued working rules for JFM to further institutionalise the programme in the working of the respective State Forest Departments.

In the present chapter, bureaucratic efficiency has been examined in the light of socio-economic changes arising out of the two participatory development programmes: watershed development Programme and joint Forest management Programme. The changes outlined as per these two programme are assessed on the basis of two separate case studies undertaken by the other scholars. In this chapter, the case study on Bureucratic efficiency on Watershed Development programme is analysed in Section-1 and the same in relation to Joint Forest Management is discussed in Section-2.

## SECTION 1

### Case Study on Bureaucratic Efficiency in Watershed Development Programme at Kashipur Block in Rayagada District

Kashipur block under Rayagada district comes under North-Eastern ghat highland agro-climatic zone of Orissa. Brown and forest soils, sandy loam, loamy and clay medium textured soils constitute the soil structure of the district. Hot and humid type of climatic conditions prevails in the district. Mean annual rainfall remains at 1597. mm and the mean temperature varies in the range of 5oC in winter and 37o in summer. In response to a proposal of Govt. of Orissa, the National Wasteland Development Board had sanctioned a number of WHS which were constructed and managed under a centrally sponsored scheme, IWDP in Kasipur block with the motive to check the adverse effect of: Rampant shifting cultivation, Large scale deforestation, Social erosion due to undulated topography, Decrease in water table, under-utilisation of land, Indifferent attitude of tribals towards development, Erratic behaviour of rain, Faulty agricultural practices.

In this background, IWDP has been implemented in this region for the construction and management of WHS. For this purpose 16 micro watersheds have been functioning since 2001-02. In each micro watershed, water harvesting structures have been created with a view for promoting irrigation and other social utilities (ASCO, Rayagada). Runoff water which, in earlier years were allowed to flow in natural drainage system, now stored in tanks and reservoirs for irrigation. The present case study deals with the following objectives.

- To assess the cropping pattern in study area due to IWDP promoted WHSs. Cropping pattern are analysed in the light of land use pattern, crop shifting, yield rate, return per hectare of land, use of HYV seeds and cropping intensity.
- To examine the level and extent of food security of the people those who are directly reaping the benefits of WHSs created under IWDP Programme and those who are living outside the project area.
- To assess and compare the incidence and intensity of poverty among the people living both in the project area and outside the project area on the basis of the estimated food poverty line.

## Materials and Methods

The study is based on primary data collected from a random sample of 200 households selected from four villages- 2 villages from the project area and 2 other villages outside the project area of Kashipur block in Rayagada district with the aid of structured questionnaire. Equal numbers of households (50 hhs) were selected from each village on the basis of Systematic Random Sampling with a random start. The survey was conducted during January 2005. The expenditure data and some information of the household relates to the recent past especially during the last month and the information on cropping pattern, HYV area coverage, yield rate, return from land etc. relates to the last one year. The household data is purely based on the memory recall of the respondent with cross checking from co-residents. The mode of data collection involves: (i) direct questioning of household head and other members; (ii) extracting data from the participant observations; and (iii) interviewing of selected informants.

To examine the impact of IWDP water harvesting structures on cropping pattern, food security and level of deprivation; two villages namely Upparjhire and Jodipai under two micro watersheds and two villages namely Baharpadamajhi and Kosabera, the adjoining villages where IWDP programme is not in operation were selected purposively. This is done for comparing the chosen variable of the project area with that of the corresponding figures of non- project area which will provide a clear picture of the impact WHS on cropping pattern, crop intensity, food security and the incidence and intensity of poverty. In another way, adjoining non-project areas acted as a surrogate for the project Area when the IWDP project was not implemented.

Food insecurity was examined in the light of Task Force Methodology i.e. if the per capita per day calorie intake of a person is equal to or exceeds 2400 calories, the person is food secured. The per capita calories intake separately calculated for project areas and non-project areas indicates the changes in food-security of the people arising due to the creation of WHS. To analyse the extent of food insecurity of the people in this region, the distribution of households over 8 calorie class are computed. GT index is calculated to know the extent of shortfall of calories intake among all the food insecure households. To assess the changes in the level of deprivation and to measure the incidence and severity of deprivation due to WHSs, the food poverty line is estimated using the cost of calorie functions as per the methodology adopted by Greer and Thorbeck. In addition to this, ratio and percentage analysis is mostly employed to examine the impact of WHS on cropping pattern.

## Impact of WHS on Agriculture

### *Cropping Pattern*

Cropping pattern means the proportion or percentage area under different crops during a agricultural year. The change in cropping pattern reflects a change in the proportion or percentage of area under different crops from one agricultural year to another agricultural year or from one region to another region in the same year. The prevalent cropping pattern in a particular area is the cumulative results of the past and present decisions of the people or a community, availability of agricultural inputs, the policy of the govt. and their agencies etc. The impact of WHS on cropping pattern in the study is analysed comparing the pattern of crop shifting, yield rate of crops, gross return per hectare, proportion of HYV cropped area to gross cropped area and the cropping intensity of the project area with that of the non-project area.

### *Crop Shifting*

Before IWDP intervention, the farmers were mostly growing the traditional crops like paddy, ragi, minor millets, horse gram and hill grams. Due IWDP water harvesting structures, now farmers are cultivating cash crops and vegetables. A comparison of different crops in project area with that of the non-project area shows that in non-project area, the percentage of area utilised to produce traditional crops like paddy and minor millets is higher than the project area. Minor variation is observed in case of pulses like horsegram, hillgram, blackgram and kating. It is further observed that except beans, project area farmers are specialised in producing varieties of vegetables like potato, onion, brinjal, garlic, cauliflower, cabbage, radish, ladiesfinger etc which are not cultivated in non-project areas. Besides, the percentage of area diverted to cash crops like nizer, mustard and sugarcane is much higher in project areas than non- project areas (Table-1). It is striking to note that the farmers in project area are replacing traditional crops by vegetables and cash crops which is definitely a positive impact of WHS in the diversification of cropping pattern.

**Table 1: Cropping Pattern and Crop Shifting in the Project Area and Non-project Area During 2004**

| *Crops* | *Land utilisation in project area (in acres.)* | *Land utilisation in non-project area (in acres.)* |
|---|---|---|
| Paddy | 38.68 (26.22) | 14.3 (31.60) |
| Ragi | 24.82(16.82) | 9.25 (20.44) |
| Minor-millet | 9.65 (6.54) | 8.7 (19.22) |

| | | |
|---|---|---|
| Maize | 5.6 (3.79) | 00 |
| Horsegram | 4.35 (2.94) | 1.2 (2.65) |
| Hillgram | 00 | 0.5 (1.10) |
| Blackgram | 3.5 (2.37) | 1.5 (3.31) |
| Kating | 9.75 (6.61) | 2.6 (5.74) |
| Beans | 2.05 (1.38) | 3.85 (8.50) |
| Peanut | 2.05 (1.38) | 0.25 (0.55) |
| Potato | 6.6 (4.47) | 00 |
| Onion | 5.75 (3.89) | 00 |
| Brinjal | 4.0 (2.71) | 00 |
| Pumpkin | 3.05 (2.06) | 0.45 (0.99) |
| Cucumber | 0.6 (0.40) | 0.2 (0.44) |
| Garlic | 0.5 (0.33) | 00 |
| Tomato | 8.2 (5.55) | 0.35 (0.77) |
| Cauliflower | 0.7 (0.47) | 00 |
| Cabbage | 3.8 (2.57) | 00 |
| Radish | 0.45 (0.30) | 00 |
| Nizer | 12.1 (8.20) | 2.0 (4.41) |
| Ladiesfinger | 0.7 (0.46) | 00 |
| Sugarcane | 0.25 (0.16) | 00 |
| Chilli | 0.35 (0.23) | 0.1 (0.22) |
| | 147.5 (100.00) | 45.25 |

N.B: Figures in parenthesis represents percentage to the column total.

## Yield Rate

The yield rate of different crops cultivated in the catchment areas of WHSs and percentage deviation in the yield rate in project area to non-project area was calculated and presented in Table-2. The results of the yield rates indicate that these rates are higher in the project areas than non-project areas for almost all crops. The percentage deviation in yield rates of different crops also reflects a significant change in the yield rate of the project area over the yield rate of non-project area without WHS. It is observed from the results given in Table- 2 that in all the reported crop except pumpkin, cucumber and peanut the yield rate increases. The marginal yield rate is the maximum in the case of horsegram. The crops for which marginal yield rate is more than 200% includes all types of cereals and pulses. Of course in the case of black-gram, it is 194.59 which is very much closer to 200 percent. In case of peanut, cucumber and pumpkin, there is negative marginal change in yield rate. It may be due to the fact that these are traditional vegetables among the tribals of the area under study. Due to WHS, these traditional vegetables have been replaced by other valuable vegetables in the project area. Besides, the new vegetables like potato, onion, brinjal, cauliflower, cabbage, radish, ladiesfinger etc. are newly cultivated by the farmers which were not cultivated before the WHSs. For these newly cultivated vegetables, the yield rate is very much satisfactory. The performance of nizer, the only cash crop of this area, the marginal change in yield rate is to the extent of 63.37 percent. Cash crops like sugarcane is also newly introduced due to WHS in the project area.

**Table 2: Change in Yield Rate of Different Crops in the Project Area and Non-project Area During 2004**

| *Sl. No.* | *CROPS* | *Yield Rate in Project Area (in quintal/ hectare)* | *Yield Rate in Non-Project (in quintal/ hectare)* | *% Deviation in Project Area* |
|---|---|---|---|---|
| 1. | Paddy | 10.71 | 3.23 | 231.57 |
| 2. | Ragi | 4.99 | 1.58 | 215.82 |
| 3. | Minor millet | 7.34 | 1.58 | 364.55 |
| 4. | Maize | 6.37 | 0.00 | -- |
| 5. | Horsegram | 8.57 | 1.64 | 422.56 |
| 6. | Hillgram | 0.00 | 0.98 | -- |
| 7. | Blackgram | 1.62 | 0.55 | 194.54 |
| 8. | Kating | 4.48 | 1.17 | 282.90 |
| 9. | Beans | 3.85 | 2.68 | 43.65 |
| 10. | Peanut | 2.80 | 4.94 | -43.31 |
| 11. | Potato | 4.69 | 0.00 | -- |
| 12. | Onion | 7.38 | 0.00 | -- |
| 13. | Brinjal | 16.67 | 0.00 | -- |
| 14. | Pumpkin | 7.80 | 8.78 | -98.0 |
| 15. | Cucumber | 2.88 | 7.41 | -61.13 |
| 16. | Garlic | 2.02 | 0.00 | -- |
| 17. | Tomato | 7.15 | 6.35 | 12.59 |
| 18. | Cauliflower | 16.76 | 0.00 | -- |

| | | | | |
|---|---|---|---|---|
| 19. | Cabbage | 9.97 | 0.00 | -- |
| 20. | Radish | 3.84 | 0.00 | -- |
| 21. | Nizer | 2.81 | 1.72 | 63.37 |
| 22. | Ladiesfinger | 11.11 | 0.00 | -- |
| 23. | Sugarcane | 14.82 | 0.00 | -- |
| 24. | Chilli | 3.88 | 1.23 | 215.47 |

Note: Computed from field data.

## Cultivation of HYV Crops

Table 3 reveals that in non-project area about 91 percent of the crops grown are local varieties and a very small proportion of crops around 9 percent are HYV varieties. On the other hand, in project area even though the share of HYV crops is higher than non-project area, it is less than the proportion of local crops cultivated in project area. The performance of cropping pattern in terms of the use of HYV crops is not satisfactory on the ground that still there exists tremendous potential for the adoption of HYV seeds.

**Table 3: Proportion Cropped Area Under Local and HYV Crops**

| *Sample* | *% Share of HYV* | *% Share of local* |
|---|---|---|
| Project Area | 40.12 | 59.88 |
| Non-Project Area | 8.75 | 91.25 |

## 2.5 Cropping Intensity

The cropping intensity, as the percentage change in gross cropped area to the net area sown, for project areas and non-project area is estimated at 1.33 and 1.18 respectively. Even though the yield rate and gross revenue per hectare, in two areas vary significantly, but there is negligible difference in the cropping intensity. This is due to the fact that agricultural operations are mostly confined to early Kharif and late Kharif but hot extended to Rabi cultivation. It implies that, due to WHS even though there is spectacular change in per hectare yield rate and per hectare gross revenue, but agriculture has not yet been all seasoned. It is because the WHSs are dried up during summer and could not be used up for Rabi irrigation but provides sufficient irrigation during Kharif. It is also observed that due to WHS crop failures and drought like situations have been completely avoided at least during Kharif in the project area but the situation is different in non-project areas.

## 2.6 Changes in Gross Return Per Hectare of Land

Crop-wise gross return (total revenue) per hectare of land in project area in comparison to the Gross return per hectare of land in non-project area indicates marginal changes arising due to WHS. These crop-wise marginal changes are analysed by calculating the percentage deviation in gross revenue in project area with that of the non project area. It is revealed from the figures given in Table-4 that for all the reported crops, the gross return per hectare of land in project area is higher in comparison to the non-project area except cucumber.

**Table 4: Change in Gross Return (Total Revenue) Per Hectare from Different Crops in the Project Area and Non-project Area During 2004**

| *Sl.* | *CROPS* | *Gross Return per hect. Project Area (in Rs.)* | *Gross Return per hect. in Non-Project Area (in Rs.)* | *% Deviation in Project Area* |
|---|---|---|---|---|
| 1. | Paddy | 4281.31 | 1257.45 | 240.47 |
| 2. | Ragi | 2007.45 | 634.46 | 216.40 |
| 3. | Minor millet | 2186.91 | 486.05 | 349.93 |
| 4. | Maize | 3742.49 | 0.00 | — |
| 5. | Horsegram | 9261.08 | 1976.00 | 368.67 |
| 6. | Hillgram | 0.00 | 948.48 | — |
| 7. | Blackgram | 2328.86 | 790.40 | 194.64 |
| 8. | Kating | 3209.73 | 1098.20 | 192.27 |
| 9. | Beans | 3831.51 | 3012.76 | 27.17 |
| 10. | Peanut | 3929.11 | 1482.00 | 165.12 |
| 11. | Potato | 2360.67 | 0.00 | — |
| 12. | Onion | 4368.68 | 0.00 | — |
| 13. | Brinjal | 10917.40 | 0.00 | — |

| | | | |
|---|---|---|---|
| 14. Pumpkin | 2073.99 | 1756.44 | 18.07 |
| 15. Cucumber | 864.5 | 1852.50 | -53.33 |
| 16. Garlic | 2025.40 | 0.00 | — |
| 17. Tomato | 3614.94 | 2893.43 | 24.93 |
| 18. Cauliflower | 11167.93 | 0.00 | — |
| 19. Cabbage | 5752.50 | 0.00 | — |
| 20. Radish | 494.00 | 0.00 | — |
| 21. Nizer | 3627.43 | 2395.90 | 51.40 |
| 22. Ladiesfinger | 3046.33 | 0.00 | — |
| 23. Sugarcane | 2964.00 | 0.00 | — |
| 24. Chilli | 5575.14 | 1852.50 | 200.95 |

*Note:* Computed from field data.

The marginal change in gross return per hectare of land is more than 200 percent for all the cereals. In case of horse gram it is the maximum of 368 percent among all the crops grown in project area. For vegetables the marginal change in gross return varies from 18 percent to 200 percent.

## 3. Poverty and Food Security

Poverty in Orissa is a predominately rural phenomenon and about 90 percent of the poor living in the rural areas of the state. The overall incidence of poverty in the state is about 48 percent. In the southern region of the state, which includes undivided districts of Koraput, Kalahandi and Phulbani, the incidence of poverty is about 87.2 percent. In this region, the incidence of poverty is about 92.4 percent on ST households, 89 percent on SC households and 77.7 percent on other households. One peculiarity of this region is the incidence of chronic poverty, which is about 64.7 percent. This is a great challenge to the planners and policy makers of the state.

### 3.1 Poverty

For assessing the impact of the WHSs on the incidence of poverty and the standard of living of the people of this region, we have estimated the food poverty line at Rs. 118.70 per capita per month using the cost of calorie function and the methodology followed by Greer and Thorbeck. The food poverty line is found to be suitable for backward areas especially for tribal areas for measuring the standard of living as the noon-food consumption expenditure is meagre compared to food expenditure. On the basis of food poverty line, we have estimated the GT index separately for households living in the project area and for households living in the non-project area to examine the intensity or severity of poverty. The poverty measure- GT index is a relative measure of income shortfall which is an indicator of an individual's relative degree of deprivation. The incidence of poverty is 86% in project area and 97% percent in non-project area. The GT index is 0.2157 for people living in the project area and 0.3316 for people living in the non-project area. This indicates the severity of poverty is much higher, hence, the standard of living is very poor in the non-project area compared to the project area.

### 3.2 Food Security

Although Orissa is self sufficient in food grains, reports of hunger and starvation pour in regularly from the southern region of the state. In the recent past, Kasipur block came to lime light for starvation deaths, chronic poverty and hunger. The reason why people die of starvation and hunger is not because of non-availability of food but because of they can not afford to purchase food that is available. At this point PDS has important role to play to provide food security. As this region has become very much prone to starvation deaths, chronic poverty and hunger, thus it is imperative to study the changes in food security due to WHSs, while analysing the multifaceted impacts of WHS. The inability of a person to eat enough food, stay active and lead a healthy life comes under the purview of food insecurity (M.S. Swaminathan Research Foundation, 2001).

In this study, we have estimated 'food insecurity' on the basis of the recommended average level of per capita daily intake of 2400 calories for the rural areas (The task Force on projections of Minimum needs and Effective consumption demand, 1993). The households satisfying this criterion are identified as Food secure households. For assessing the impact of WHSs on food security, the percentage of Food secured households in the project area was compared with that of the non-project area. The marginal changes in food security due to WHS are the excess of food secured households in project area with that of the non-project area.

**Table 5: Distribution of Households on the Basis of Calorie Class**

| *Panel* | *Calorie class* | *% of HHs in project area* | *% of HHs in Non-Project Area* |
|---|---|---|---|
| A | 300-600 | 9.52 | 10.45 |
| | 600-900 | 23.81 | 27.68 |
| | 900-1200 | 22.19 | 24.34 |
| | 1200-1500 | 19.06 | 20.42 |
| | 1500-1800 | 11.90 | 7.20 |
| | 1800-2100 | 6.38 | 4.34 |
| | 2100-2400 | 7.14 | 5.57 |
| | Total | 100.00 | 100.00 |
| B | 2400 & above | 16.00 | 0 |
| | | | Combined GT index = 0.2315 |

*Note:* Calculated from field data.

As per our estimates only 16 percent of the households in project area are food secure households. It in hearting to note that all the households in non-project area are food insecure households (Table 5, Panel b). Thus our analysis indicates that WHSs have been able to promote food security only to the extent of 16 percent, which is the difference of the percentage of food secure households in project area to that of the non-project area. Table-5 (panel-a) depicts the percentage distribution of food insecure households in terms of per capita daily calorie-intake classes in project Area in relation to the non- project area. The distribution clearly indicates that the percentage of highly food insecure households are higher and comparatively less insecure households are lower in the non-project area and reverse is the case in the project area.

## Conclusion

WHSs as a source of irrigation have positive influence on cropping pattern by means of crop shifting from traditional crops to more valuable cash crops. Perceptible changes are noticed in the yield rate of almost all the crops and the gross return per hectare of land is found satisfactory. Adoption of HYV seeds, though moderate, still marginal changes are encouraging. Cropping intensity is not changed because water retaining capacity of WHS is confined to Kharif only. During summer, as WHSs are dried up, Rabi crops can't be grown. Overall impact of WHS on cropping pattern though encouraging still there is very large scale food insecurity to the extent of 84 percent in the project area and 100 percent in the non-project area. It is because of the faulty consumption pattern of the tribals and they are exploited in the product as well as labour market. IWDP Project Implementing Agencies (PIAs) and the NGOs are to be involved for the dedication of liquor among the tribals and beneficiaries in the project area are to be taught on savings in the line of micro finance and grain banks. These motivational aspects deserve special attention for the food security of the tribals.

## SECTION 2

## A Case Study on the Bureaucratic Efficiency in the Joint Forest Management Programme Implemented in Ganjam District

The development of the Joint Forest Management Programme in India is based on the National Forest Policy of 1988 which emphasized the involvement of the village communities living close to the forests in protection and development of forests and development of the degraded forest land Besides, National Forest Policy, 1988 laid emphasis on natural regeneration, preserving biodiversity and adopting management practices that help the local people. The translation and implementation of this basic policy for protecting forests and environment and reducing the poverty level of rural masses paved the way for the emergence of Joint Forest Management(JFM). The Government of India, Ministry of Environment and Forests issued an enabling Joint Forest Management Resolution on June 1st,1990 for the active involvement of village community living close to the forests and development of degraded forest land. The main features include the following: It was integrated with socio-economic realities in a multiple cultural and ethnic setup embarking on a path of productivity and prosperity through sustainable use of scarce natural resources. In the year 1995, the Resolution was slightly modified to involve women and landless households as well as usufruct sharing by the communities. To provide legal back up to JFM committees, it was further revised on February 21.2000.Orissa is among the 27 states to implement the JFM programme and it is the third highest state to implement the JFM program more vigorously after Madhya Pradesh and Andhra Pradesh (Planning Commission 2001). The village forest protection committee is called Vana Surakshya Samittee(VSS). In the light of the NFP 1988, JFM has been considered to be the right policy intervention for ensuring livelihood improvement of the forest dependent poor in Orissa, who are underorganised and underprivileged due to their poverty, ignorance and impoverishment. By the end of June 2004, there were 7358 VSSs in the 49 forest divisions covered under 8 forest circles in Orissa. The total forest area covered under the JFM program stands at 8, 03,807.16 hectares (See Table 3).

**Table 3: Circle-wise Performance of JFMs in Orissa (As on 30.06.2004)**

| *Sl. No.* | *Circles* | *No of* | *Assigned Forest area (in Hectares)* |
|---|---|---|---|
| 1 | Angul (Angul, Athagarh, Athamallik, Cuttack, Dhenkanal, Satakosia WL | 632 | 72454.58 |
| 2 | STR-Baripada (Baripada, Balasore WL, Bhadrakh WL, Karanjia, Rairangapur, STR Baripada | 702 | 168707.41 |
| 3 | Berhampur (Baliguda, Baudh, Berhampur, | 1235 | 108261.79 |

| | | | |
|---|---|---|---|
| | Ghumsar-N, Ghumsar-S, Paralakhemundi, Phulbani) | | |
| 4 | Bhawanipatana (Bolangir-E, Bolangir-W, Kalahandi-N, Kalahandi-S, Khariar, Sunabeda (WL) | 1526 | 116966.61 |
| 5 | Bhubaneswar (Chandaka-WL, Chilika-WL, City Forest, Khurda, Mahanadi-WL, Nayagarh, Puri-WL, Rajnagar-WL) | 219 | 26772.65 |
| 6 | Koraput (Jeypore, Koraput, Malkanagiri, Nawarangapur, Rayagada) | 1292 | 91252.04 |
| 7 | Rourkela (Banai, Deogarh, Keonjhar, Keonjhar-WL, Rourkela, Sundargarh) | 1083 | 119149.41 |
| 8 | Sambalpur (Bamara-WL, Basuguda, Hirakud-WL, Rairakhol, Sambalpur-N, Sambalpur-S) | 669 | 100332.69 |
| | Total | 7358 | 803807.16 |

*Source:* Office of the PCCF, Orissa, Bhubaneswar

N.B.: Names in Parenthesis are the respective forest Divisions.

## 2.2 Need and Objectives of the Study

Orissa is one among the major states to implement the JFM program and till date more than 7000 VSSs have been formed in different Forest Circles in Orissa. It is right time to assess different impacts of this program towards the sustainable rural development in Orissa. In this background, present study analyses the socio-economic, environmental changes in the JFM areas of Orissa.

## 2.3 Study Approach and Methodology

For analyzing the changes due to JFM program 16 VSS villages under Digapahandi Forest Range and Gundibira VSS under Surada Forest Range are considered. The socio-economic and the environmental changes are assessed on the basis of a number of selected indicators. The performance of the selected indicators is outlined on the basis of primary data obtained from the people in the selected VSS areas with the help of Focus Group Discussion (FGD) and rapid Rural Appraisal (RRA). The changes due to JFM program is measured by comparing the values of the selected variables during the

Post –JFM period with the corresponding figures during the Pre-JFM period. In this study 9 VSSs—Pipiliguda, Narasinghagada, Gaida, Moreibadi, Raipur, Patrachudi, Harina, Kandhakhududi, Kamalpur under Digapahandi Forest Range and Gundibira under Surada Forest Range are considered.

### 3.1 Socio-economic Impacts of JFM Program

To examine the socio economic changes due to Joint Forest Management, the indicators like incidence of small farmers, marginal farmers, agricultural laborers, forest dependent households and the type of migration etc are analyzed. The details of the socio-economic indicators and their changes due to the present JFM program are shown in table-4.

**Table 4: Socio-economic Changes due to JFM**

| *Sl. No.* | *Indicators* | *Pre-VSS* | *Post-VSS* | *Net change (% deviation)* |
|---|---|---|---|---|
| 1 | Incidence of Small Farmers (% of households to the total households)/VSS | 19.08 | 19.08 | Nil |
| 2. | Incidence of marginal farmers (% of households to the total households)/VSS | 28.24 | 42.74 | 51.25 |
| 3. | Incidence of agricultural Labor Households (% of households to the total households)/VSS | 48.85 | 34.35 | -29.66 |
| 4. | Incidence of forest dependent Households (% of households to the total households)/VSS | 38.16 | 3.81 | -90.01 |
| 5. | Migration of adult laborers (No. of persons)/VSS | 25 | 55 | 120.00 |
| 6. | Migration of child laborers (No. of child laborers) /VSS | 15 | 6 | -60.00 |
| 7. | Dropout rate[1] | 40.81 | 12.72 | -68.83 |
| 8. | Low birth weight babies 2/Year (Weighted average separately calculated during Pre-VSS and Post-VSS) | 1.5 | 1.0 | -33.33 |

| | | | |
|---|---|---|---|
| 9. Livestock Population (in nos./VSS) | | | |
| No. of cows | 300 | 500 | 66.66 |
| No. of bullocks | 12 | 60 | 400.00 |
| No. of goats/sheep | 60 | 200 | 233.33 |
| 10. Average milk production (liters/month/VSS) | 900 | 1500 | 66.66 |
| 11. Shops (nos/VSS.) | 2 | 5 | 150.00 |
| 12. Artisan households (nos/VSS.) | 5 | 10 | 50.00 |
| 13. Women entrepreneurship (no. of SHGs/VSS) | 0 | 6 | - |

N: B: All the figures in Col 3and col 4 are the averages of all the JFM villages in the study.

*Source:* Computed from the field data

It is revealed from table 4 that during the post VSS period, the incidence of small farmers remaining constant, and the incidence of marginal farmers has increased by 51.25 percent and this has reduced to 30 percent for agricultural labor households. This indicates that most of the agricultural labor households during the pre-VSS period have moved upward and become marginal farmers. Similarly the incidence of forest dependent households, those who are exclusively dependent on forests for their livelihood is significantly reduced and the extent of reduction is around 90 percent. It is inferred that there has been better occupational mobility and better awareness for the protection of forest. Besides, these households are pressurized by JFM members not to be engaged in illicit timber trafficking, collection and sales activity for some better economic activity. As a result, out-migration from the VSS area to Surat Textile Mills has increased to the extent of 120 percent. Similarly, livestock activities during the post–VSS period have also increased sharply. The increase in the livestock population such as the number of cows, bullocks, goats, and sheep has increased by 66%, 400%, and 233.33% respectively. During the pre-VSS period there were no Holstein cows in the JFM villages which are reported to be around 10 per village.

The average milk production during a month in the VSS

area has increased by 66 percent. The increase in the number of shops, artisan households and women entrepreneurship speaks about the occupational mobility of the forest dependent households. There is increasing tendency among women to be associated with micro finance activities through Self Help Group Program. For instance, the JFM formed SHG comprising of forest fringe women members of Gundibira VSS under Ghumsar (South) forest Division have produced beautiful market -oriented Seasons Greetings and Wall Calendars.

Even the human development indicators like drop-out rate and the incidence of low birth weight babies has reduced. This is due to the increased awareness consequent upon the health camps and literacy campaigns periodically undertaken in the VSS areas.

### 3.2 Environmental Impacts of JFM

The environmental impacts of JFM are examined by analyzing the indicators associated with soil conservation, moisture conservation and improved environment. Indicators like number of tube wells, number of dug wells, both type of wells remaining dry during summer, mean temperature during summer etc have been studied to understand and assess the extent of moisture stress created by the adjoining forestry now covered under the JFM program. It is revealed from Table 5 that though there has not been any increase in the mean number of tube wells per village but the no of dug wells are increased by 14.28 percent. The no of tube wells are not increased because tube wells in the villages are installed by the Govt. It is also found that the no of tube wells and wells remaining dry during summer have decreased to the extent of 50 and 60 percent respectively. Improvement in the water table is also reported to the extent of 25 percent. Thus, overall performance with respect to moisture conservation is found satisfactory. Mean temperature during the peak summer is also reported to be declining in the micro climates adjacent to the forests covered under the JFM programme.

For assessing soil conservation, indicators like amount of sand and stone transported from VSS sit e to construction sites are studied. Due to the active involvement of the VSS people, such type of transportation has been checked by 50-100 percent. As a result, soil erosion in forest areas has been prevented. This is definitely a significant outcome of VSS.

Environmental protection due to VSS efforts are analyzed by studying the variables like the amount of timber transported from the forest areas to outside, number of days of forest firing during summer, number of picnics arranged at the VSS sites. It is found that during the post VSS period; there have been around 99 percent reduction in the amount of timber transported and 90 percent reduction in forest firing. There has been 6 times increase in the number of days picnic arranged in the VSS sites.

Thus against this background the environmental promotion role of VSS is profound. Effective utilization of Minor Forest Produces (MFPs) is also one of the important objectives of JFM. It is reported that in the study area MFPs are not found much. However it is found that the number of households engaged in leaf plate making is sufficiently increased and the increase is as high as 400 percent.

**Table 5: Environmental Changes due to JFM**

| *Sl. No.* | *Indicators* | *Pre-VSS* | *Post-VSS* | *Net change (% deviation)* |
|---|---|---|---|---|
| 1. | No. of tube wells per JFM village | 6 | 6 | 0 |
| 2. | No. of wells per JFM village | 7 | 8 | 14.28 |
| 3. | No. of tube wells remaining dry during summer | 2 | 1 | -50.00 |
| 4. | No. of wells remaining dry during summer | 8 | 5 | -60.00 |
| 5. | Mean Water table during summer | 25′ | 20′ | -25.00 |
| 7. | Mean temperature during Summer | 43o | 40o | 12.5 |
| 8. | Stone transported (No. of truckloads/week) | 20 | 0 | -100:00 |
| 9. | Red sand transported (No. of truckloads/week) | 8 | 0 | -100.00 |

| | | | | |
|---|---|---|---|---|
| 10. | Timber transported (No. of bicycle-loads/week) | 500 | 2 | -99.6 |
| 11. | Households engaged in leaf plate making | 2 | 10 | 400.00 |
| 12. | Picnics arranged at VSS site | 2 | 15 | 650.00 |
| 13. | Forest Firing (No. of days during summer) | 20 | 2 | -90.00 |

N: B: All the figures in Column 3 and 4 is the average of all the JFM villages considered in this study.

*Source:* Computed from the field data, 2006.

### 3.3 Perceived Benefits of the JFM Program

VSS wise the benefits as perceived by the people is shown in Table-6. The different benefits as perceived by the villagers include present as well as future benefits. The whole range of benefits as summarized in the following table necessarily speaks about the sustainability symptoms.

**Table 6: Benefits of the JFM Programme as Perceived by the Villagers**

| *Sl.No.* | *Name of the VSS* | *Project Benefits* |
|---|---|---|
| 1 | Pipiliguda | • Forest loss prevented to the extent of 70 percent<br>• Increased availability of fuel and timber in future.<br>• Increase in the income of the forest dependent households.<br>• More employment<br>• Increased no of goats and sheep in the village among the forest dependent households<br>• More plantation consciousness |
| 2 | Narasinghagada | • Profuse regeneration of bamboo trees<br>• More number of wild animals reported in the jungle.<br>• Complete prevention of forest fire. |
| 3 | Gaida | • Reduction in illicit transportation of timber.<br>• Reduction in the incidence of forest fire.<br>• Profuse regeneration of bamboo trees<br>• In-migration of elephants.<br>• Increased availability of fodder.<br>• Increased concentration of wild animals |
| 4 | Moreibadi | • Increased stall feeding practice for the cattle among the villagers. |

| | | |
|---|---|---|
| | | • In migration of wild animals<br>• Flow of streams from forests<br>• Reduction of top soil erosion due to the soil and moisture conservation works.<br>• Reduction in illicit stone transportation.<br>• Reduction in the incidence of the forest dependent households.<br>• Massive regeneration of trees.<br>• Once extinct, reappearance of the wild species like gunduri. |
| 5 | Raipur | • More interest to go for plantation in the private lands<br>• Restricted open grazing<br>• Introduction of crossbred cows.<br>• Prevention of forest fire.<br>• Additional income of the households due to increased off farm employment opportunities. |
| 6 | Patrachudi | • Sufficient availability of firewood.<br>• More awareness for maintaining the forest<br>• Better quality of life due to the convergence of programmes like WATSAN and Swajaladhara with the JFM works |
| 7 | Harina | • Massive regeneration o0f bamboo trees.<br>• Multiple regeneration of plants.<br>• More availability of MFPs.<br>• Reduction in the illicit stone transportation<br>• Plenty availability of fire wood, Timber and fodder as future benefits. |
| 8 | Kandhakhududi | • Increased stall feeding practices.<br>• Indigenous cows being replaced by she-buffaloes<br>• Increased milk production.<br>• Plenty availability of firewood and bamboo as future benefits |
| 9 | Kamalpur | • Place is first becoming a tourist place.<br>• More inflow of tourists for arranging picnic parties in the VSS jungles.<br>• Flow of streams from forest.<br>• Reduction in the top soil erosion.<br>• In migration of elephants.<br>• Due to increased fodder availability in the forest, wild animals are not interfering in crop lands |
| 10 | Gundibira | • Future availability of fuel and timber.<br>• Sustainability of forest resources.<br>• Scenic beauty of the forest. |

*Source:* Field Survey, 2006.

### 3.4 Problems in the Smooth Functioning of the JFM Program

Table 7 shows the various limitations of the JFM program as perceived by the villagers. The major limitations as revealed in the following table include non adoption of PRA exercise while formulating the JFM program, non maintenance of records and registers and non completion of micro plan. It is reported that as the various functionaries of the executive body of the VSS are illiterates they can't provide attention towards the preparation of micro plan and maintaining records and registers. Another major limitation of the JFM program is that in around 30 percent of the VSSs, the various functionaries like president and secretary are not transparent to the member households regarding the fund flow under the VSS program.

**Table 7: Limitations of Joint Forest Management as perceived by the JFM Households**

| *Sl No* | *Type of limitations* | *No of Reporting JFMs (%)* |
|---|---|---|
| 1 | Non completion of Micro plan | 40 |
| 2 | Delay in the sanction of funds | 30 |
| 3 | Non adoption of PRA Exercise | 60 |
| 4 | Conflict among the households | 20 |
| 5 | More interference of Grampanchayat functionaries in JFM matters | 20 |
| 6 | VSS functionaries do not provide information to the members | 30 |
| 7 | Records/Registers are not up to date. | 60 |
| 8 | Forest Officials dominate over JFM matters | 30 |
| 9 | Minimum wage Payment is violated | 10 |
| 10 | Fictitious Records/Registers | 10 |

## 4.0 Concluding Remarks

With the introduction of the JFM program there has been sufficient preservation, protection and maintenance of forest resources, marked improvement in the socio-economic life of the forest fringe households and positive changes in the environmental aspects. A fraction of the agricultural labor households have escaped from poverty. Meat and milk production in the VSS areas have increased. There has been satisfactory soil and moisture conservation due to the forest protection and forestation activities undertaken by the VSS. Added to such benefits, ground water table has improved, forest firing prevented bio-diversity in VSS areas enhanced and occupational mobility improved to a satisfactory level. Effective utilization of MFPs is also reported. People's involvement in the protection of forests is tremendously pro-active. However issues like delays in the sanction of funds, non-transparency of the VSS functionaries, insufficient provision of training and exposure visits for the members have partially hindered the progress. Considering that there is tremendous scope for sustainable rural development of the forest fringe households through the JFM program, all types of constraints associated with such type of governance should be removed.

## NOTES

1. Out of the enrolled children in primary schools, proportion of children has left school in between the education sessions. The mean drop-out rate of the preceding five years to the introduction of the VSS and succeeding 3 years has been considered.
2. Babies weighing less than 2,500 grams during birth are considered Low Birth Weight (LBW).

# 7

# Role of Bureaucracy in Economic Development: A Case Study of Micro Finance and Public Distribution System in Orissa

In this chapter, an attempt has been made to further assess the role of bureaucracy in the matters relating to micro finance programme and public distribution system. It is to note that micro finance is an alternative financial mechanism, largely promoted among the rural poverty stricken households through Self Help Group Programme. SHG s are alternatively called saving and credit groups and the type of credit dealt in these groups are known as Micro Credit. From the practical point of view, micro credit, Self Help Groups and saving/ credit groups are viewed synonymous. The origin of the SHG concept can be traced back to the year 1976, when Prof Mohammad Yunus of Chitagong University set up the Grameen Bank experiment in Bangladesh for alleviating poverty. The Grameen Bank concept went on to become a huge success and the model swayed many microfinance institutions across the world. In an epoch making statement after receiving the Nobel Prize for peace in the year 2006 he stated that by the year 2030 poverty would be terminated every where in the world and the scars of poverty would be found in the museum only. This shows the strength of the model for terminating poverty. When a group of poor or disadvantaged people come together on their own (voluntarily) with the clear objectives of bringing about positive changes in the situation in which they find themselves in, through self help and self reliance, such a group is called Self Help Group(SHG).A saving and credit groups is a specialized form of SHG, where the group members agree to form themselves into a group and function in an organized manner with the specific objective of pooling their savings so as to able to give credit to its members for meeting their consumption and production needs. The main objectives of groups are to improve the economic and social status of the members in terms of their needs and interests.

SHGs are always self managed. However to make the SHG programme thorough and efficient many-a-times an out side agency called Self Help Promoting Institution(SHPI) may be a bank or NGO or local youth club, Anganwadi center (AWC), panchayat authorities or any other person necessarily acting as facilitator provides required guidelines towards a better start. So many multilateral donor agencies like OXFAM, CARE(India), ACTION AID, etc have been providing catalytic support for the promotion and expansion of micro credit programme with the objective of bringing about positive changes in the socio economic status of poverty ridden households. Institutions like National Bank for Agriculture and Rural Development (NABARD), Small Industries Development Bank of India (SIDBI), Rashtriya Mahila Kosh (RMK) promoted under Ministry of Women Child Development, Government of India have been patronizing this programme.

Even under Watershed Development Programmes, there is clear provision of providing support base to the SHGs consisting of members coming from landless households. Again there is lot of fund diversion to the watershed development programmes in the KBK districts[1] in Orissa as per the provision of Long-Term Action Plan.

On the other hand, Indian Public Distribution System

(PDS) started before independence when people suffered from serious food shortages. The government of India imported food grains and supplied them through rationing. After independence, the Public Distribution System came into existence replacing the earlier ad hoc rationing system and its coverage was confined to urban areas and to a few food deficit states (Reddy and Rao 2004). In the 1950s and 1960s, the country was experiencing serious national level food shortages and the upward pressure on food prices was particularly acute in urban areas. Given India's emerging post-independence economy with the incompleteness or absence of agricultural markets in most regions, that have persisted till today, this pattern of regional specialisation of agricultural production has meant that the Central Government needed to setup and operate an administered price system of public procurement and distribution to ensure that areas which are food grain deficient got the required produce for their population. In this backdrop, the Food Corporation of India (FCI) was setup under the Food Corporation Act, 1964 in order to fulfil the objectives like price support operations for safeguarding the interest of the farmers, distribution of food grains throughout the country for Public Distribution System and maintaining satisfactory level of operational and buffer stock of food grains to ensure national food security. The PDS as it evolved during this period probably served the dual purpose of containing the upward pressure on prices of staple food and protecting the urban consumers, even if it did not serve the interests of rural poor (Radhakrishna and others, 1997). The Food Policy of India had been encouraging the producers by fixing support prices to the food grains and supplying the grains at a subsidised fixed price to the vulnerable sections of the population throughout the year. In 1985, specially subsidised food grain production was introduced in all the tribal blocks covering about 57 million people. PDS was later expanded under the Revamped Public Distribution System (RPDS), which was introduced on 1st January 1992 in 1752 blocks, which were covered under Desert Development Programme (DDP), Drought Prone Areas Programme (DPAP) and certain Designated Hill Areas (DHA). When RPDS was free for APL and BPL classes, there was criticism in many quarters. By that time, it was felt that the marginal impact of PDS seemed to be a function of the universality of its coverage, i.e. every household, irrespective of income could have an entitlement card and use it to obtain food grain. This non-targeted nature of the PDS meant that grain did not often reach the poorest in the society and gave way to Targeted Public Distribution System (TPDS). In operation from 1997 that attempted to segment the population in two categories, such as, Above Poverty Line (APL) and Below Poverty Line (BPL), the latter group obtaining food grains and essential items at a lower price. For the first time the dual price, policy was introduced in TPDS in order to benefit the poor more through Public Distribution System. Both the Central Government and State Government participate in the procurement and distribution of food grains.

To understand the pattern of functioning of the above mentioned schemes and their effectiveness two case studies are analysed. The case Study on the functioning of Micro financing programme is shown in section-1. The second case study relates to the functioning of Public Distribution System and its efficiency in conned with ensuring food security shown in Section-2. The first case study was undertaken in Nawaramgapur district in Orissa whereas for the second case study entire KBK districts in Orissa were considered.

## SECTION 1

### Effectiveness of Bureaucracy for Oromoting Rural Development through Micro Finance Programme

The District Nawarangpur is located in the Southwest corner in Orissa between 820 to 830 East longitudes and 190 to 200 North latitude was created due to the bifurcation of undivided Koraput district in 1992. It is bounded by the state of Chhatisgarh to the west and north and the districts of kalahandi and Rayagada to the east and Koraput to the South. The district has a total geographical area of 5294 Sq KMs, which is 3.4 percent of the state geographical area. The agro climatic region of the district consists of eastern ghat highlands and western undulating lands, while 9 out of the 10 blocks are included in the former category, only one block, i.e., Chandahandi comes under the later category. The district covers 1.18 lakh hectares of high land, 0.38 lakh hectares of medium land and 0.29 hectare of low land. The total population of the district according to 2001 census is 10.26 lakhs against 368.05 lakhs of the state population. Between 1991 and 2001 the decinial growth rate of population in Nabarangpur district was 20.3 percent compared to the state average of 15.9 percent. The density of population per sq km in the district stands at 194 as against the state average of 236 per sq km (Govt of Orissa 2005). The district, being a part of the KBK districts, where the centrally sponsored KBK Scheme is currently being implemented to break the deadlock of multifundamental backwardness such as tribal areas, hill areas and drought prone areas backwardness. Chronic poverty and the large scale malnutrition are the characteristic features of the district. To alleviate poverty and reduce the incidence of malnutrition, a number of strategies have been implemented from time to time. Microfinance through SHGs is one such attempt in this direction.

Analysis of 55th round and 60th round National Sample Survey Organisation (NSSO) data projects Orissa being the poorest state in India. Further region wise disaggregation of NSSO data indicates that the southern region of the state is the acute poverty zone in the state (Hann and Dubey 2001, Planning Commission 2007). The southern districts comprise of undivided Koraput, Phulbani and Bolangir district in orissa. The KBK Long Term Action Plan (LTAP) highlighted the incidence of rural poverty in KBK districts is even more than eighty percent. In this background, the promotion and expansion of micro credit programme in this region is extremely genuine. The study carried out in Nabarangpur district, one of the KBK districts, is of immense importance in view of the following reasons. Micro credit programme has special relevance for improving the socio-economic status of the rural households.

- Nabarangpur is a part of southern orissa where there is the highest incidence of poverty and food insecurity.

- A number of watershed development programmes under the schemes like Integrated Watershed Development Programme (IWDP), Employment Assurance Scheme (EAS), Revised Long Term Action Plan (RLTAP), Drought Prone Areas Programme (DPAP), etc are currently being implemented in all the 11 blocks of the district.
- The district is tribal dominated.

## Objectives of the Study

In the fitness of the above, the present study examines the following objectives.

- To assess the activities and functioning of groups in terms of their operation, activities, strategies, problems and future scope.
- To ascertain the impact of self help groups on the socio-economic status of its members.
- To suggest steps, measures and changes required for making the SHG program more viable and sustainable.
- To understand the role of micro credit program on poverty and food security in Nabarangpur district.

During the last 4 years there has been continuous progress of SHG programme in the district. By the end of 2005-06 there are 10548 SHGs as against 6110 SHGs in the year 2002-03. During the corresponding period, there has been around 4- fold increase in the total deposits made by all the SHGs. Average deposit and average bank loan per SHG stand at Rs. 7695/- and Rs. 24832/- respectively which were Rs. 3964/- and Rs. 11771/- in the year 2002-03. It is to note that more than 60 percent of the SHGs in the district have been linked with banks. Details of the progress of the SHG program in the district are shown in the following Table-1.

**Table 1: Progress of SHGs in Nabarangapur District**

| *Year* | *No of SHGs* | *Total Deposits of all SHGs (Rs. in lakhs)* | *Average deposit per SHG* | *No of SHGs availed bank loan* | *Amount of bank loan (Rs in lakhs)* | *Average Bank loan per SHG* |
|---|---|---|---|---|---|---|
| 2002-03 | 6110 | 242.23 | 3964 | 1120 | 131.83 | 11771 |
| 2003-04 | 7680 | 382.43 | 4980 | 1604 | 279.52 | 17426 |
| 2004-05 | 9513 | 583.06 | 6129 | 3715 | 781.84 | 21045 |
| 2005-06 | 10548 | 811.67 | 7695 | 4079 | 1022.88 | 24832 |

*Source:* DRDA (2006).

## Methodology

The study intends to analyze the effectiveness of tribal SHGs promoted under watershed areas in Nabarangpur district. Thus, purposefully 4 tribal dominated blocks where watershed programme is currently being implemented are selected. Out of the selected 4 blocks, 2 blocks come under DPAP watershed and the other 2 blocks come under IWDP watersheds and from each block 10 SHGs are selected on the basis of Simple Random Sampling. Again from each selected SHG, 5 members are randomly selected with the aid of lottery method. Thus the total sample size consists of 200 SHG members in the watershed Areas. By compiling their socio-economic status with their past, the immediate preceding time when they were not the members of any SHG, the marginal changes are analyzed. The very process of examining the present socio-economic change due to SHG by comparing the relevant variables when they were not the members of any SHG is known as longitudinal Analysis. For analyzing data required statistical tools are employed. The Sampling design for the present study is presented in table 2.

## Table 2: Sampling Design

| *Sl No* | *Blocks* | *Gram Panchayat* | *No of SHGs selected* | *No of Respondents* |
|---|---|---|---|---|
| 1 | Papadahandi | Semeli | 10 | 50 |
| 2 | Nabarangapur | Pujariguda | 10 | 50 |
| 3 | Chandahandi | Koilimunda | 10 | 50 |
| 4 | Kosagumuda | Kosagumuda | 10 | 50 |
| Total | 4 Blocks | 4 GPs | 40 SHGs | 200 Respo-ndents |

## Impact of SHGs on Agriculture/Allied Activities

Like any backward and tribal region, the economy of Nawarangapur district is basically agrarian. In an agrarian setting, it is quite obvious to understand the nature of progress of agriculture as it provides the livelihood support to the masses. The reported SHGs are found in the watershed areas. Thus, in addition to their inner potentiality, SHGs are also appropriating the benefits from watershed program. Again, due to the convergence of watershed program with the other development programs in the district, a good deal of development intervention is continuously taking place in the study area. As a part of the convergence program, farm equipments like tractors, kerosene pump sets, crossbred cows have been provided to SHG families under Swarna Jayanti Gram Swarojgar Yojana (SGSY). As per the analysis of data it is found that during the pre SHG period, there were no tractor and pump set in the SHG families. By the end of 2005-06, there are 247 tractors/power tillers among the SHG families and 6.5 percent of the SHG families own pump sets for irrigation purposes. The pattern of agricultural change in the Study area by analyzing selected indicators is presented in table-3.

The provisioning of crossbred cows has not only replaced the indigenous cows by crossbred cows but also boosted milk production in the study area. It is to note that due to the efforts of the SHG families in watershed areas, 8000 litres of milk are daily collected by Orissa Milk Producers Federation (OMFED).

**Table 3: Performance of Selected Indicators Relating to Agricultural Change**

| *Sl No* | *Selected indicator* | *Pre SHG Period* | *Post SHG Period* | *No. of times change (Column4/ Column 3)* |
|---|---|---|---|---|
| 1 | 2 | 3 | 4 | 5 |
| *1 | No of tractors and the power tillers among the SHG Households | 0 | 247 | -NA- |
| *2 | Percentage of SHG Households owning Kerosene pump sets for irrigation Purposes | 0 | 6.5 | -NA- |
| 3 | Daily milk collection by the District milk union (in litre) | 1189 | 8000 | 6.72 |
| 4 | Maize production as percentage to total cereal production | 10 | 55 | 5.5 |
| 5 | Vegetable cultivation as percentage to GCA | 5 | 25 | 5.0 |
| 6 | Gross Revenue per Hectare(in Rs) | 6000 | 60000 | 10 |
| 7 | Important cash crops | Niger (1 crop) | Cashew nut, sugarcane, maize (3 crops) | 3 |
| 8 | High Yielding Varities of crops as percentage to Gross Cropped Area (GCA) | 20 | 80 | 4 |
| 9 | Supplementary income from poultry (as Percentage share in the annual Household income) | 10 | 20 | 2 |

*Source:* *1and *2 District Rural Development Agency, Nabarangapur, Oths-computed from field data.

Maize production has been sufficiently encouraged. Previously it was hardly 10 percent of the Gross Cropped area (GCA). Now it has increased to more than 50 percent of the GCA. Considering increased revenue potential of maize, farmers of the district are fast replacing the traditional crops by maize. In addition to maize, farmers are also producing high valued, market oriented vegetables. Traditionally, nizer was the only cash crop produced by the farmers of the study area. Now due to the encouragement and technical support given under watershed programme has encouraged farmers to cultivate a number of cash crops like Maize, sugarcane and cashew nut. As per District Rural Development Agency (DRDA) sources, to boost livelihoods security to rural people in the district, 20,000 hectares of cashew nut plantation has been created by the Government and subsequently handed over to local SHGs for maintenance and their livelihood security. Simultaneous increase of Plantation crops, horticultural crops, increased milk production, meat production and shifting from traditional crop production to cash crops indicates a good deal of crop diversification possible due to the efforts of the SHGs in watershed areas.

**Impact on Household Income**

For analyzing the impact of SHG programme on income the annual household income of the SHG households during the pre SHG period was compared with the corresponding figures during the post SHG period. Annual income wise, households are divided into 5 categories as lower (Rs0-5000), lower income (Rs5000-10000), middle (10000-15000), upper middle (Rs15000-20000) and higher (>Rs20000) groups. It is found that due to SHG programme, there is reduced incidence of lower and lower middle income groups. During the post SHG period, the percentage of lower and lower income groups stand at 20.0 and 26.5 percent respectively as against 47.0 and 39.5 percent at the time of pre-SHG period. On the other hand, the proportionate share of middle, upper middle and higher income groups has increased in comparison to their respective incomes during the Pre SHG period. This indicates that the households from the lower income group have improved to higher income. The mean annual household income is calculated to be Rs 10,450/-against the corresponding figure at Rs. 6175/- during the Pre SHG period (Table-4).

**Table 4: Changed Income Pattern**

| *Sl. No.* | *Income Class (In Rs)* | *No. of Households (pre-SHG)* | *Post SHG(No. of Households)* |
|---|---|---|---|
| 1 | 0-5000 | 44(47.0) | 40(20.0) |
| 2 | 5000-10000 | 79(39.5) | 53(26.5) |
| 3 | 10000-15000 | 17(8.5) | 68(34.0) |
| 4 | 15000-20000 | 6(3.0) | 27(13.5) |
| 5 | >20000 | 4(2.0) | 12(6.0) |
| | Total | 200(100.0) | 200(100.0) |
| | Mean Income(Rs) | 6175 | 10450 |

N: B: Figures in bracket is the percentage to the corresponding column total

*Source:* Computed from field data.

## Impact on Household Consumption

The incidence of poverty, food insecurity, hunger and malnutrition are frequently noticed in the tribal areas of KBK districts in Orissa. It is in this background KBK Long Term Action Plan was formulated by the central Government of India in the year 1993-94. Microfinance through SHGs is a broad based approach basically aiming at reducing the incidence of extreme poverty and malnutrition. In this context, while analyzing the impact of SHG program, an attempt has been made to assess the changes in the consumption pattern of cereals and pulses. The distribution of households on the basis of Per Capita Per Day Consumption (PCPDC) of cereals is shown in Table-5 and the PCPDC of pulses in Table-6.

It is found that the mean PCPDC of cereals is estimated to be 343.5 Gms during post SHG period which was 296.0 Gms in pre SHG period. For around 68 percent of the households PCPDC of cereals was less than 300 Gms during pre SHG period. But due to the SHG activities and consequently the increased income, there is marginal improvement in the consumption pattern of cereals because only 30 percent of the households, now, are found with less than 300 Gms of PCPDC of cereals. More than 50 percent of the households are reported to be PCPDC of cereals between 300 to 400 grams.

**Table 5: Changed Consumption Pattern of Cereals**

| Sl No. | PCPDC of Cereals (in gms) | Pre SHG (No. of Households) | Post SHG (No of Households) |
|---|---|---|---|
| 1 | 100-200 | 27(13.5) | 6(3.0) |
| 2 | 200-300 | 109(54.5) | 21(26.5) |
| 3 | 300-400 | 28(14.0) | 104(52.0) |
| 4 | 400-500 | 17(8.5) | 54(11.0) |
| 5 | >500 | 19(9.5) | 15(7.5) |
| | Total | 200(100.0) | 200(100.0) |
| | Mean PCPDC of cereals | | 296.0 343.5 |

N: B: Figures in bracket is the percentage to the corresponding column total

*Source:* Computed from field data.

Similarly, the mean PCPDC of pulses is found to be 56.6 grams during the post SHG period as against 34.1 grams during the pre-SHG period. For more than 60 percent of the households, PCPDC of pulses was less than 40 Gms during the pre SHG period. Even during the post SHG period the consumption pattern of pulses has not changed significantly. Presently, during the post SHG period, still for about 40 percent of the households, PCPDC of pulses is found to be less than 40 Gms (Table-6).

**Table 6: Changed Consumption Pattern of Pulses**

| Sl No. | PCPDC of pulses (in gms) | Pre SHG (No of Households) | Post SHG (No of Households) |
|---|---|---|---|
| 1 | 0-20 | 67(33.5) | 38(19.0) |
| 2 | 20-40 | 58(29.0) | 43(21.5) |
| 3 | 40-60 | 42(21.0) | 76(38.0) |
| 4 | 60-80 | 33(16.5) | 14(7.0) |
| 5 | 80-100 | 0 | 16(8.0) |
| 6 | >100 | 0 | 13(6.5) |
| | Total | 200(100.0) | 200(100.0) |
| | Mean PCPDC of pulses | 34.1 | 56.6 |

N: B: Figures in bracket is the percentage to the corresponding column total

*Source:* Computed from field data.

## Impact of SHGs on Food Poverty and Food Security

The mean changes in the Per Capita Per Day Consumption (PCPDC) of cereals and pulses have significant bearing with Per Capita Per Day Calorie. Per capita per day household calorie is a sufficient indicator to measure food poverty and food insecurity. If a household is having per capita per day calorie less than 2400 calories in rural areas, then, the household is identified as food insecure household (Planning Commission 1977). For examining the per capita per day calorie, the calorie equivalents of daily food consumption adjusted with family size is calculated. The calorie equivalents are obtained as per the prescriptions made by the Task Force Methodology (Sixth Five Year Plan Technical Note). The distribution of households on the basis of per capita per day calorie intake is shown in Table-7.

**Table 7: Changed Calorie Pattern**

| *Sl No.* | *Calorie Class* | *Pre SHG (No of Households)* | *Post SHG (No of Households)* |
|---|---|---|---|
| 1 | 800-1000 | 6(3.0) | 0 |
| 2 | 1000-1200 | 4(2.0) | 0 |
| 3 | 1200-1400 | 7(3.5) | 2(1.0) |
| 4 | 1400-1600 | 8(4.0) | 11(0.5) |
| 5 | 1600-1800 | 37(18.5) | 7(3.5) |
| 6 | 1800-2000 | 38(19.0) | 14(7.0) |
| 7 | 2000-2200 | 43(21.5) | 33(16.5) |
| 8 | 2200-2400 | 21(18.5) | 46(23.0) |
| 9 | >2400 | 36(18.0) | 97(48.5) |
| | Total | 200(100.0) | 200(100.0) |

N: B: Figures in bracket is the percentage to the corresponding column total

*Source:* Computed from field data.

The above table reveals that more than 80 percent of the households during the pre SHG period were food insecure households due to less than 2400 per capita per day calorie. The corresponding figure has changed during the post SHG period and only 52 percent of the households are food insecure. Thus, micro finance activities through SHGs have significant potential in reducing the incidence of poverty and food insecurity. Kennedy (2004) points out that a household is said to be hunger affected if the per capita per day calorie is less than 1800 calorie. On this basis 33 percent of the households were hunger affected during the pre SHG period. However during the post SHG period the incidence of hunger affected households has drastically come down to 5 percent. As KBK districts are mostly hunger prone, SHG program could be a solution because of its potential in arranging extra purchasing power by means of employment opportunities. Empirical studies undertaken in this area point out that lack of off-farm employment opportunities significantly contribute the incidence of food poverty and hunger in this region (Panda 2006).

## Impact on Consumption Expenditure

Monthly household expenditure adjusted with the household size determines the Monthly Per Capita Consumption Expenditure (MPCE). MPCE is supposed to be a good indicator to assess the household consumption pattern. It is revealed from the statement given in Table 8 that the MPCE of the SHG households have been classified under five categories-Rs. 100-200, Rs. 200-300, Rs. 300-400, Rs. 400-500, and >500. By comparing the MPCE of the pre SHG period with the post SHG period, it is found that the MPCE for around 82 percent of the households were between Rs. 100-200 and the rest between Rs 200-500. However during the post SHG period, only 13 percent of the households are between Rs. 100-200 as MPCE and about 77 percent between Rs. 200-500 as MPCE. For about 10 percent of the households MPCE has increased to more than Rs. 500/-.

**Table 8: Changed Consumption Expenditure**

| *Sl No.* | *Monthly per Capita Consumption Expe-nditure (in Rs)* | *Pre SHG (No of Households)* | *Post SHG (No of Households)* |
|---|---|---|---|
| 1 | 100-200 | 163(81.5) | 27(13.5) |
| 2 | 200-300 | 24(12.0) | 119(59.5) |
| 3 | 300-400 | 11(5.5) | 31(15.5) |
| 4 | 400-500 | 2(1.0) | 5(2.5) |
| 5 | >500 | 0 | 18(9.5) |
| | Total | 200(100.0) | 200(100.0) |

N: B: Figures in bracket is the percentage to the corresponding column total

*Source:* Computed from field data.

## Impact on Household Assets

Asset concentration among the households is an important indicator to measure the level of development. Due to increase income consequent upon crop diversification and micro finance activities, conversion of cash into material assets is sufficiently reported in the study area. On the basis of sample data it is found that during pre-SHG period, only 2 percent of the SHG households had semi-pucca houses which has been changed to 30 percent during the post SHG period. The incidence of cell phones is found among 15 percent of the households. Due to the convergence of watershed program with district WATSAN program, 15 percent of the SHG households have access to latrine facility in their house. The incidence of bicycles (65%), motor cycles (22%), electricity connection to houses (42%),television(38%), households having bank accounts in public sector banks (47%)is currently reported as against the corresponding figures at 8%, 1%, 3%, 2%, 2% respectively during the pre-SHG period (see table-9). This indicates the increased consumerism and development in rural areas propelled by the forces of micro finance activities.

**Table 9: Changed Asset Density (in % of households)**

| Sl No. | Type of Assets | Pre SHG | Post SHG |
|---|---|---|---|
| 1 | Semi-pucca Houses | 2 | 30 |
| 2 | Diesel/pump set | 0 | 6.5 |
| 3 | Access to latrine facility | 0 | 21 |
| 4 | Bicycles | 8 | 65 |
| 5 | Motorcycles | 1 | 22 |
| 6 | Electricity connection to houses | 3 | 42 |
| 7 | Television | 2 | 38 |
| 8 | Bank A/Cs other than SHG A/C | 2 | 47 |

*Source:* Computed from field data.

## Concluding Remarks of Case-1

Simultaneous increase of Plantation crops, horticultural crops, increased milk production, meat production and shifting from traditional crop production to cash crops indicates a good deal of crop diversification which have become possible due to the efforts of the SHGs in watershed areas. The households from the lower income groups have improved to higher income. The mean annual household income is calculated to be Rs. 10,450/-against the corresponding figure at Rs. 6175/- during the Pre SHG period. It is found that the mean PCPDC of cereals is estimated to be 343.5 Gms during post SHG period which was 296.0 Gms in pre SHG period. Similarly, the mean PCPDC of pulses is found to be 56.6 grams during the post SHG period as against 34.1 grams during the pre-SHG period. Micro finance activities through SHGs have significant potential in reducing the incidence of poverty and food insecurity. During the post SHG period, only 13 percent of the households are between Rs. 100-200 as MPCE and about 77 percent between Rs. 200-500 as MPCE. For about 10 percent of the households MPCE has increased to more than Rs. 500/-. Due to increase income consequent upon crop diversification and micro finance activities, conversion of cash into material assets is sufficiently reported in the study area. This indicates increased consumerism and development in rural areas propelled by the forces of micro finance activities. Because of the tremendous socio-economic merits associated with this program, the sustainability of the program is of crucial importance. Convergence of the rural development programs with the micro finance programme could lead to sustainability.

## SECTION 2: A Case Study on the Role of Bureaucracy on the Effectiveness of Public Distribution System

Though PDS is essentially aimed at equitable distribution of essential commodities at reasonable prices to the poorer sections, now-a-days it is frequently reported that, a large number of people do not lift their quota of wheat and rice from PDS shops. Traders lift this unutilised quota of food grains and sell them at higher prices in the open market. In most cities, and quasi-urban areas PDS has been reduced to a source of extra income for traders. Evidences are also found that, the selection of BPL households is mostly based on false premises. Most often rich people stand more advantageous so far as Targeted Public Distribution System (TPDS) is concerned. In newspapers, it is also reported that so many cardholders use their ration card for sales/mortgage, as if the ration card is a liquid asset. Due to the inter-play of so many reasons, the role of PDS as a guarantor of food security is largely debated. Orissa is the poorest state in India having around 50 per cent of its people below the poverty line as per official estimates, coupled with poverty as high as 60%-70% of its people living at critical calorie intake. Analysis of anthropometric indicators and symptoms of clinical malnutrition in a number of studies indicates that Orissa is the most vulnerable on the ground of poverty, hunger, and malnutrition.

Again the KBK region in Orissa is the most backward region in India, which is having the highest incidence of poverty and the share of BPL population as estimated by Hann and Dubey (2004) on the basis of 55th round NSS data, is more than 80 percent. Probably this is due to high concentration of tribal population in this region. Existing literature supports the view that areas having higher incidence of poverty are significantly affected by food insecurity. At this backdrop, PDS should play effectively to reduce the incidence of poverty and food insecurity. Keeping in view the poverty and related backwardness of the KBK region, it has been decided to incorporate this case study for analyzing the effectiveness of bureaucracy for providing safeguards against poverty and food insecurity. This case study is based on primary data obtained from 200 households of four selected blocks in the three of the KBK districts in Orissa. The three selected KBK districts are Koraput, Rayagada, and Kalahandi. The selected blocks are Th Rampur (Kalahandi District), Kashipur in Rayagada district and Boipariguda in Koraput district. The analysis of the primary data is reported in the following section

## Coverage of Beneficiaries under PDS Scheme

The distribution of households according to different PDS schemes point out that out of 210 sample households, 17 households (8.09%) in all Blocks are not covered under any scheme which signifies the fact that they are non-poor households. The block-wise coverage of beneficiaries under different PDS schemes is shown in Table 10.

**Table 10: Distribution of Households as per Different PDS Schemes**

| *Sl No.* | *Blocks* | *No. of Beneficiaries under different PDS Schemes* | | | |
|---|---|---|---|---|---|
| | | *Antyodaya Yojana* | *Annapurna Yojana* | *BPL Rice Scheme* | *Total* |
| 1. | Kashipur | 8 (11.11) | 0 (0.00) | 64(88.86) | 72(100.00) |
| 2. | Th.Rampur | 6(11.66) | 0(0.00) | 45(88.25) | 51(100.00) |
| 3. | Jeypore | 6(20.66) | 0(0.00) | 23(79.34) | 29(100.00) |
| 4. | Boipariguda | 5(12.40) | 0(0.00) | 36(87.60) | 41(100.00) |
| | Total | 25(12.95) | 0(0.00) | 168(87.04) | 193(100.00) |

*Source:* Computed from the field data.

N.B: Figures in Parenthesis represents percentage to row total.

It is observed from the above table that in all Blocks, except Jeypore Block, around 12% of the PDS beneficiaries are covered under Antyodaya Yojana and the remaining 88% are covered under BPL provisions. At Jeypore Block, the percentage share of beneficiaries under Antyodaya and BPL rice provisions stand at 20.66% and 79.34% respectively. No beneficiary is reported to have been covered under Annapurna Yojana.

## Regularity of Purchase

Generally, PDS quota of essential commodities is fixed on monthly basis, that means each beneficiary household is required to lift his quota on every month. By analysing the survey data it is found that around 60% of the households do not lift their quota regularly. The type of purchase of PDS items on the basis of regularity for the reporting Blocks is shown in Table 11.

**Table 11: Distribution of Households on the Basis of Regularity of Purchase**

| *Sl No* | *Blocks* | *Regularity of Purchase* | | *Total* |
|---|---|---|---|---|
| | | *Yes* | *No* | |
| 1. | Kashipur | 26(36.14) | 46(63.86) | 72(100.00) |
| 2. | Th.Rampur | 15(29.41) | 36(70.56) | 51(100.00) |
| 3. | Jeypore | 8(27.56) | 21(72.44) | 29(100.00) |
| 4. | Boipariguda | 10(24.35) | 31(75.65) | 41(100.00) |
| | Total | 59(30.56) | 134(69.45) | 193(100.00) |

*Source:* Computed from the field data.

From the above table it is found that 69.45% of the respondent households in all the blocks under the study are not regularly purchasing from PDS. As maximum as 75.65% of the PDS beneficiaries at Boipariguda Block are not regularly lifting their quota from PDS. The percentage share of beneficiaries who are not lifting their quota regularly stands at 72.44%, 63.86%, 70.56% for Jeypore, Kashipur, and Th.

Rampur respectively. From this discussion, it follows that a significant majority of the PDS beneficiaries are not regularly lifting their quota.

### Reasons for Not Lifting the Allotted Quota

The amount of rice allotted under the different schemes like Antyodaya Yojana and BPL Rice is 35kg and 16kg per month respectively. A household fails to lift its allotted quota due to several reasons. As per our survey, the main reasons for which the allotted quota is not lifted by the concerned households include: unawareness of the time of availability of PDS items, dealers' refusal to sanction the full quota, timely non-availability of money, low quality of PDS items, insignificant difference between PDS and open market prices etc. Scheme-wise the reasons for not lifting the full quota is presented in Table 12.

**Table 12: Reasons for Not Lifting the Quota**

| *Sl* | *Reasons for not lifting the quota* | *Antyodaya Yojana* | *BPL R Provisions* | *Total* |
|---|---|---|---|---|
| 1. | Unaware of the time of availability of PDS items | - | 1(0.76) | 1 (0.74) |
| 2. | Dealer's refusal to sanction the full quota | 2 (28.57) | 8 (6.25) | 10 (7.46) |
| 3. | Timely non-availability of money | 3(42.85) | 78(61.47) | 81(60.44) |
| 4. | Low quality PDS items | - | 5(3.95) | 5(3.75) |
| 5. | Insignificant difference between PDS and open market prices | - | 2(1.57) | 2(1.45) |
| 6. | Rent/Sale/Mortgage & Gifting of the ration cards | 2(28.57) | 33(25. 96) | 35(26.11) |
| 7. | Total | 7(100.00) | 127(100.00) | 134(100.00) |

*Source:* Computed from the field data.

N. B: Figures in parentheses represent percentage to column total.

As per the previous table 12, 134 households (69.45 %) of the PDS covered households are not regularly lifting the quota. Out of 25 households covered under Antyodaya Anna Yojana (Table 7.1), 28.0 % of the households are not lifting their quota regularly. Similarly, around 76 % of the households covered under BPL rice scheme are not regularly lifting their respective PDS quota. Perhaps the comparative lower price of rice under Antyodaya Yojana has encouraged the households to lift their full quota. It is revealed from the above table that timely non-availability of money is the dominant reason for the irregularity of lifting their quota. Sale, mortgage and gift of ration card is also a major factor for which around 26 % of the beneficiaries are unable to lift their monthly PDS quota. In the study area it is reported that many households have sold or mortgaged their ration cards to meet some of their urgent expenses like medical expenses, annual house repair/maintenance and to meet some religious expenses. It is reported that beneficiaries under both the schemes are utilising their ration cards as liquid assets and face value of Antyodaya card is greater then the BPL card.

## Status of Ration Card

In the study area ration card is being used as a liquid asset i.e. very easily it is being converted into money by means of sales, mortgage, rent etc. Thus, on the basis of these factors, it is very essential to study the present status of the ration card for the households covered under PDS.

**Table 13: Distribution of Respondents on the Basis of the Status of Ration Card**

| *Sl.* | *Status of* | *Block-wise Distribution of Households* | | | | *All* |
|---|---|---|---|---|---|---|
| *No.* | *Ration Card* | *Kashipur* | *Th. Rampur* | *Jeypore* | *Boipariguda* | *Block* |
| 1. | It is with the household | 64 (88.86) | 40 (78.45) | 26 89.65) | 31 (75.60) | 161 (80.41) |
| 2. | It is with dealer | 2 (2.77) | 9 (17.64) | 2 (6.85) | 2 (4.87) | 15 (7.77) |
| 3. | It is lost (1.36) | 1 (0.00) | 0 (3.44) | 1 (2.45) | 1 (1.55) | 3 |
| 4. | It is sold (0.0) | 0 (0.0) | 0 (0.0) | 0 (7.37) | 3 (1.55) | 3 |
| 5. | Gift/mortgage | 5 (6.94) | 2 (3.92) | 0 (0.00) | 4 (9.75) | 11 (5.65) |

*Source:* Computed from the field data.

N. B. figures in parenthesis present percentage to column total.

It is understood from table 13 that around 80 percent of the PDS households, presently, have their ration card. The rest 20% of card holders have either left it with the dealer, sold/mortaged or lost. This figure is around 25 percent at Boipariguda, around 21 % in Th. Rampur, 11% for Kashipur and 10% in Jeypore. Mishandling of ration card is maximum reported in terms of keeping the ration card with the dealer followed by gift/mortgage, loss and sale of ration etc.

## Annual Purchase of Rice from PDS

The pattern of annual purchase of rice from PDS by the households covered under PDS is furnished in table 7.5, for the blocks under study. Block-wise average purchase of PDS rice is also shown to get some insight on the quantity difference in allotted quota and lifted quota. Out of 193 PDS households, 26 households (13.47%) of the households have never lifted their PDS quota during the Reference Period. Thus, the purchase behaviour of 167 households is shown in table 14.

**Table 14: Distribution of Households on the Basis of Annual Off-take of Rice from PDS**

| *Quantity of rice purchased annually from PDS (in kgs.)* | *Block-wise Distribution of Households* | | | | |
|---|---|---|---|---|---|
| | *Kashipur* | *Th.Rampur* | *Jeypore* | *Boipariguda* | *All Blocks* |
| 0-50 | 2 | 2 | 6 | 13 | 23 |
| 50-100 | 9 | 9 | 2 | 4 | 24 |
| 100-150 | 11 | 9 | 8 | 1 | 29 |
| 150-200 | 37 | 22 | 4 | 2 | 65 |
| 200-250 | 0 | 0 | 1 | 1 | 2 |
| 250-300 | 0 | 0 | 0 | 0 | 0 |
| 300-350 | 0 | 0 | 0 | 1 | 1 |
| 350-400 | 1 | 0 | 0 | 0 | 1 |
| >400 | 7 | 6 | 6 | 3 | 22 |
| No. of households | 67 | 48 | 27 | 25 | 167 |
| Average Annual purchase | (177.98) | (171.87) | (76.85) | (117.0) | (166.91) |
| Average monthly purchase | 14.83 | 14.32 | 6.40 | 9.75 | 13.91 |

*Source:* Computed from the field data.

It is revealed from the statement given in table 7.5 that in all blocks under study on an average each household lifts 166.91 kg of rice from PDS. This figure is found to be the highest at Kashipur Block (177.98 Kg) followed by Jeypore (176.87 kg), Th. Rampur (171.87 kg.) and Boipariguda (117.0 kg). Average monthly purchase comes around 14 kg. for Th. Rampur and all blocks, for Kashipur the figure is around 15 kg. Jeypore shows the lowest purchase of 6.40kg, whereas this figure for Boipariguda is 9.75 kg. only. On any measure this indicates poor performance of PDS an acute poverty of the people under study.

### Difference in the Allotted Quota and Lifted Quota

The extent of difference in the allotted quota and lifted quota during the reference year is calculated to assess the amount not lifted from PDS. It is observed from table 15 that as maximum as 45 percent of the sample households in all the blocks are having the extent of difference in the range 75-100 kg per annum followed by the ranges 50-75 kg (15.18%), 25-50kg (12.56%) 20-25 kg. (12.04%). It is quite disheartening to note that only 13.61% of the households lift their full quota. The extent of difference in the range 75-100 kg. Stands the highest percent in Kashipur (61%) followed by Th. Rampur (54.90%), Jeypore (34.48%) and the lowest in Boipariguda (7.89%).

**Table 15: Distribution of Households on the basis of difference in allotted quota and lifted quota**

| *Sl. No.* | *Difference in Allotted quota and lifted quota* | *Block-wise Distribution of Households* | | | | *All Block* |
|---|---|---|---|---|---|---|
| | | *Kashipur* | *Th. Rampur* | *Jeypore* | *Boipariguda* | |
| 1 | 0 | 6 (8.3) | 4(7.84) | 3(10.34) | 13(34.21) | 26 (13.61) |
| 2. | 0-25 | 2 (2.73) | 2(3.92) | 6(20.68) | 13(34.21) | 23(12.04) |
| 3. | 25-50 | 9(12.32) | 9(17.65) | 2(6.89) | 4(10.52) | 24(12.56) |
| 4. | 50-75 | 11(15.81) | 8 (15.68) | 8(27.58) | 2(5.26) | 29(15.18) |
| 5. | 75-100 | 45(61.00) | 28(54.90) | 10(34.48) | 3(7.89) | 86(45.02) |
| 6. | >100 | 10.00 | 0 (0.00) | 0(0.00) | 3(7.89) | 3(1.57) |
| | Total | 73 (100.00) | 51 (100.00) | 29 (100.00) | 38 (100.00) | 191 (100.00) |

*Source:* Computed from the field data.

N.B: Figures in parentheses shows percentage to column total.

## Expenditure on PDS as a Percentage to total Cereal Expenditure

PDS expenditure as a percentage to cereal expenditure of the sample households in the blocks under study is shown in table 16. It is found that maximum number of households (27.22%) spends 0-10 percentage of their cereal expenditure on PDS rice and minimum of 1.58 percent of the households spend 90-100 % of their cereal expenditure on PDS rice and for around 14% of the households, PDS expenditure to cereal expenditure varies in the range of 60-100%. Actually, these groups of households are more dependents on PDS.

**Table 16: Household Expenditure on PDS as a percentage to Cereal Expenditure**

| *Sl. No.* | *% Expenditure on PDS* | *Block-wise Distribution of Households* Kashipur | Th. Rampur | Jeypore | Boipariguda | *All Block* |
|---|---|---|---|---|---|---|
| 1 | 0-10 | 7 (9.72) | 5(9.80) | 13(44.82) | 27(69.23) | 52(27.22) |
| 2. | 10-20 | 12(16.66) | 10(19.60) | 7(24.13) | 6(15.38) | 35(18.32) |
| 3. | 20-30 | 14(19.44) | 8(15.68) | 3(10.34) | 2(5.13) | 27(14.13) |
| 4. | 30-40 | 13 (18.05) | 5(9.80) | 2(6.89) | 4(10.26) | 24(12.56) |
| 5. | 40-50 | 8(11.11) | 8(15.68) | 2(6.89) | 0(0.00) | 18(9.42) |
| 6. | 50-60 | 4(5.55) | 3(5.88) | 1(3.44) | 0(0.00) | 8(4.18) |
| 7.. | 60-70 | 3(4.16) | 6(11.76) | 0(0.00) | 0(0.00) | 9(4.71) |
| 8. | 70-80 | 6(8.33) | 1(1.96) | 1(3.44) | 0(0.00) | 8(4.18) |
| 9. | 80-90 | 5(6.94) | 2(3.92) | 0(0.00) | 0(0.00) | 7(3.66) |
| 10. | 90-100 | 0(0.00) | 3(5.88) | 0(0.00) | 0(0.00) | 3(1.57) |
| | Total | 72 (100.00) | 51(100.00) | 29(100.00) | 39(100.00) | 191(100.00) |

*Source:* Computed from the field data.
*Note:* Figures in parentheses indicate percentage.

## Average Monthly Expenditure on PDS

Block-wise average monthly expenditure on PDS rice is shown in Table 17. It is found that in all blocks, majority of households (35%) incur Rs. 60-80 as monthly average penditure on PDS followed by Rs. 0-20 (25.13%), Rs. 40-60 (14.65%), Rs. 20-40 (12.56%). Around 38% of the households are having monthly average expenditure on PDS in the range of Rs. 0-

40 and around 54% of the studied households incur average expenditure of Rs. 0-60 on purchasing rice from PDS in all blocks.

**Table 17: Block-wise Distribution of Households on the Basis of Average Monthly Expenditure on PDS**

| *Sl. No.* | *Average Monthly Expenditure on PDS* | *Block-wise Distribution of Households* | | | | *All* |
|---|---|---|---|---|---|---|
| | | *Kashipur* | *Th. Rampur* | *Jeypore* | *Boiparig-uda* | *Block* |
| 1 | 0-20 | 7(9.58) | 6(11.76) | 9(31.03) | 26(68.42) | 48(25.13) |
| 2. | 20-40 | 9(12.32) | 9(17.64) | 2(6.89) | 4(10.52) | 24(12.56) |
| 3. | 40-60 | 11(15.06) | 8(15.68) | 8(27.58) | 1(2.63) | 28(14.65) |
| 4. | 60-80 | 38(52.05) | 22(43.13) | 4(13.79) | 3(7.89) | 67(35.07) |
| 5. | 80-100 | 1(1.36) | 0(0.00) | 0(0.00) | 1(2.63) | 2(1.04) |
| 6. | 100-120 | 7(9.58) | 6(11.76) | 6(20.68) | 2(5.26) | 21(10.99) |
| 7. | 120-140 | 0(0.00) | 0(0.00) | 0(0.00) | 1(2.63) | 1(0.52) |
| | All Households | 73 (100.00) | 51 (100.00) | 29 (100.00) | 38 (100.00) | 191 (100.00) |

*Source:* Computed from the field data.

*Note:* Figures in parentheses indicate percentage.

Maximum proportion of the households as high as 79 percent incur lowest expenditure i.e. less than Rs. 40 per month for the procurement of PDS items. On the other hand, at Kashipur block, the average monthly expenditure for procuring PDS is more than Rs. 60 for about 60 per cent of the households. More than Rs. 60 as PDS expenditure at Th. Rampur and Jeypore is reported for about 55 per cent and 35 percent of the households respectively.

## Seasonality of PDS Off-take

Month-wise mean purchase of PDS rice in the blocks under study has been referred to as the seasonality of PDS off-take. The weighted average of the mean purchases of all the blocks under study has been calculated to understand the seasonality of PDS off-take. The block-wise and month-wise mean purchase of rice from PDS is presented Table 18. Before analysing the mean purchase of PDS items it is felt necessary to understand the buying behaviour of the card holders. The buying behaviour of the card holders is analysed in table 19 in terms of the percentage of households purchasing rice from PDS during different months in a year, which is shown in Table 18. It is found that there is regularity of purchase among the card holders, i.e., every month all card holders purchase from the PDS, which is around 70 per cent at Th. Rampur. On the other hand, such behaviour among the cardholders, is found to be inconsistent at Jeypore and Boipariguda Blocks. In comparison to all the blocks, the average number of households purchasing from PDS is found to be the lowest at Boipariguda block. On an average, only 36 percent of the households purchase from PDS as against the corresponding figures at 100 per cent, 70.74 per cent, and 60.41 per cent at Kashipur, Th. Rampur and Jeypore respectively.

**Table 18: Monthwise Proportion Card Holders Purchasing Rice from PDS**

| *Sl.* | *Months* | *Block-wise proportion of households purchasing rice from PDS (%)* | | | | |
|---|---|---|---|---|---|---|
| *No.* | | *Kashipur* | *Th. Ram-pur* | *Jeypore* | *Boiparig-uda* | *All Block* |
| 1 | April | 100.00 | 70.96 | 85.00 | 62.5 | 82.36 |
| 2. | May | 100.00 | 70.96 | 72.50 | 57.5 | 79.64 |
| 3. | June | 100.00 | 70.96 | 62.50 | 40.0 | 73.86 |
| 4. | July | 100.00 | 70.96 | 56.50 | 32.5 | 71.42 |
| 5. | August | 100.00 | 69.70 | 55.00 | 52.5 | 74.26 |
| 6. | September | 100.00 | 70.96 | 52.50 | 32.50 | 70.47 |
| 7.. | October | 100.00 | 70.96 | 62.50 | 32.50 | 72.36 |
| 8. | November | 100.00 | 70.96 | 62.50 | 27.50 | 71.42 |
| 9. | December | 100.00 | 70.96 | 55.00 | 30.0 | 70.47 |
| 10. | January | 100.00 | 70.96 | 57.50 | 30.0 | 70.95 |
| 11. | February | 100.00 | 70.96 | 50.00 | 20.0 | 67.67 |
| 12. | March | 100.00 | 70.96 | 52.50 | 25.0 | 69.64 |
| Average No of households per month | | 100.00 | 70.74 | 60.41 | 36.87 | 72.77 |

*Source:* Computed from the field data.

**Table 19: Block-wise Monthly Average purchase of Rice from PDS**

| *Sl. No.* | *Months* | *Block-wise monthly average purchase of rice from PDS (in kg.s)* | | | | |
|---|---|---|---|---|---|---|
| | | *Kashipur* | *Th.Rampur* | *Jeypore* | *Boipariguda* | *All Blocks* |
| 1 | April | 13.68(10.16) | 14.26(9.77) | 11.74(14.10) | 18.12(33.85) | 14.07 |
| 2. | May | 14.61(9.61) | 13.03(10.48) | 13.41(17.02) | 5.83(11.06) | 12.81 |
| 3. | June | 15.68(9.89) | 13.44(10.26) | 16.08(15.13) | 12.94(27.04) | 14.89 |
| 4. | July | 14.04(9.76) | 12.21(10.84) | 19.57(14.20) | 20.62(20.20) | 15.17 |
| 5. | August | 16.96(13.15) | 11.68(11.73) | 18.27(13.97) | 19.00(15.95) | 16.13 |
| 6. | September | 14.83(9.46) | 12.28(14.50) | 16.86(14.49) | 16.69(12.40) | 7.84 |
| 7.. | October | 14.19(9.90) | 13.44(10.9) | 22.00(23.55) | 22.08(19.46) | 15.95 |
| 8. | November | 12.48(10.79) | 11.38(11.72) | 17.88(12.09) | 13.64(12.98) | 13.71 |
| 9. | December | 11.63(11.11) | 10.15(12.56) | 16.95(17.93) | 25.75(19.93) | 13.17 |
| 10. | January | 12.27(10.88) | 10.97(11.84) | 14.00(14.51) | 17.50(13.13) | 12.61 |
| 11. | February | 11.84(11.04) | 11.79(12.16) | 22.10(13.31) | 22.63(24.31) | 13.59 |
| 12. | March | 10.31(11.06) | 12.26(11.01) | 17.62(13.97) | 24.50(21.80) | 12.71 |

*Source:* Computed from the field data.

N.B: Figures in Parentheses indicate standard deviation of the corresponding mean value.

The mean purchase in all the blocks is found to be maximum at 16.13kg. in August followed by 15.95kg. in October, 15.17 kg. In July, 14.89kg. in June, 14.07kg. in April, 12.81kg. in May, and 13.71 kg. in November. The mean value is reported to be minimum in the month of September. The highest mean purchase of 60.96 kg., 13.44 kg., 22.10 kg., and 25.75 kg. is reported for Kashipur in the month of August, Th. Rampur in the month of October, Jeypore in the month of February and Boipariguda in the month of December respectively.

## Poverty Reducing Effects of Public Distribution System

As per the estimates, the incidence of food poverty and income poverty are found to be 83.81 and 77.14 respectivley.

The incidence of food poverty and income poverty is estimated in Table 20. As per this table, households on the basis of per capita per day calorie class, are divided into 9 calorie classes and on basis of MPCE (including food items and non-food items) are divided into 7 classes. In this table households are arranged on the basis of calorie class (vertical arrangement) and MPCE class (horizontal arrangement). Form our data it is found that there are 2 households nearest to 2400 calorie and their PCPDCs are noted to be 2397 and 2427. The corresponding MPCE on food items for 2397 calorie and 2427 calorie are chalked out to be Rs. 59.16 and Rs. 93.16 respectively. The mean value of these two MPCE is calculated to be 76.16 is defined to be food poverty line. Adding MPCE on non-food expenditure to MPCE on food expenditure, the overall MPCE for these two households calculated to be Rs. 84.32 and Rs. 140.32 respectively. Accordingly, the mean value of Rs. 112.31 is defined as income poverty line. The households who fall below the food poverty line (Rs. 76.16) and income poverty line (Rs. 112.31) are defined as the households below food poverty line and income poverty line respectively.

It is revealed from table 20 that 188 households (89.52%) are below the threshold calorie level defined as the incidence of food poverty. Similalry, the incidence of income poverty is found to be 82 per cent. In the previous chapter, with the inclusion of PDS quantity and PDS expenditure data in PCPDC and MPCE, the incidence of food poverty and income poverty had been calculated at 83.16% and 77.14 per cent respectively. Thus excluding PDS items from the cost of calorie functions the difference in food poverty and income poverty is found to be 6.35% and 4.86 % respectively. Now it may be stated that due to PDS, only 6.35 percent of households have escaped from food poverty and 4.86 per cent escaped from income poverty. Thus, the poverty reducing impacts of PDS is very much negligible.

**Table 20: Incidence of Food Poverty and Income Poverty without PDS**

| Calorie Class | Monthly Per Capita Consumption Expenditure (in Rs.) 0-100 | 100-120 | 120-140 | 140-160 | 160-180 | 180-200 | >200 | Total |
|---|---|---|---|---|---|---|---|---|
| 100-300 | 24 | 11 | 4 | 4 | 4 | 1 | 4 | 52 |
| 300-600 | 20 | 11 | 3 | 2 | 1 | 0 | 5 | 42 |
| 600-900 | 15 | 6 | 8 | 1 | 0 | 1 | 5 | 36 |
| 900-1200 | 7 | 6 | 2 | 1 | 1 | 0 | 4 | 21 |
| 1200-1500 | 2 | 3 | 0 | 0 | 0 | 4 | 2 | 11 |
| 1500-1800 | 2 | 0 | 0 | 0 | 2 | 1 | 3 | 8 |
| 1800-2100 | 1 | 1 | 1 | 1 | 1 | 2 | 2 | 9 |
| 2100-2400 | 2 | 0 | 0 | 0 | 2 | 1 | 4 | 9 |
| >2400 | 1 | 3 | 4 | 1 | 1 | 3 | 9 | 22 |
| Total | 74 | 41 | 22 | 10 | 12 | 13 | 38 | 210 |

## Concluding Remarks of Case-2

It is found that 69.45% of the respondent households in all the blocks under the study are not regularly purchasing from PDS. Out of 25 households covered under Antyodaya Anna Yojana (Table 7.1), 28.0 % of the households are not lifting their quota regularly. Similarly, around 76 % of the households covered under BPL rice scheme are not regularly lifting their respective PDS quota. Perhaps the comparative lower price of rice under Antyodaya Yojana has encouraged the households to lift their full quota. It is revealed from the above table that timely non-availability of money is the dominant reason for the irregularity of lifting their quota. Sale, mortgage and gift of ration card is also a major factor for which around 26 % of the beneficiaries are unable to lift their monthly PDS quota. In the study area it is reported that many households have sold or mortgaged their ration cards to meet some of their urgent expenses like medical expenses, annual house repair/maintenance and to meet some religious expenses. It is understood that around 80 percent of the PDS households, presently, have their ration card. The rest 20% of card holders have either left it with the dealer, sold/mortgaged or lost. It is found that in all blocks, majority of households (35%) incur Rs. 60-80 as monthly average expenditure on PDS followed by Rs. 0-20 (25.13%), Rs. 40-60 (14.65%), Rs. 20-40 (12.56%). Around 38% of the households are having monthly average expenditure on PDS in the range of Rs. 0-40 and around 54% of the studied households incur average expenditure of Rs. 0-60 on purchasing rice from PDS in all blocks. Due to PDS, only 6.35 percent of households have escaped from food poverty and 4.86 per cent escaped from income poverty. Thus, the poverty. reducing impacts of PDS is very much negligible.

# 8

# Concluding Remarks and Suggestions

It was only after independence that with the transfer of political power to Indians, a serious thought was given to development of the people. Therefore, the first and foremost challenge to the Indian administrative system of independent India was how to meet the socio-economic needs of these rural poor. This can possibly be with the introduction of rural development programmes for the rural India. Rural development is advocated today as basic strategy for economic development all over the world and India is no exception. The sheer largeness in numbers who continue to live and work in the rural areas in the developing countries, particularly India, the biggest democracy of the world, compels our attention to this important yet neglected sector of the economy. The idea of rural development originated by Mahatma Gandhi in his teachings was the champion of Gram Raj. Gandhiji succeeded in mobolishing the poor people from the villages in the unique battle for freedom by holding out before them the prospectus of better life, more dignity and honour.

Due to the absence of popular local institutions, in the beginning, the responsibility of implementation of the community development programmes was given to the steel frame bureaucracy in India. The bureaucracy failed to inspire the people's cooperation in community development programme due to its rigid approach, conservatism and lack of development attitude. As a result of its failure, on the recommendation or Balwant Rai Mehta Team, Government of India recommended the decentralization of power and authority to the popular local institution i.e. Panchayati Raj institutions. In the opinion of Late Pandit Jawaharlal Nehru both officials and non-officials and their part to play in the community development work. In India the question of development was initiated with community development programme in fifties, then in sixties the area development programme was launched, in seventies integrated rural development programme become popular and the latest emphasis now on the individual development programme realized to uplift the poorest from the level of poverty to better living.

In spite of rapid industrialization and urbanization in the country, rural areas predominate and there is no remarkable diversification of rural economy with desirable level of social and economic changes in a backward state like Orissa. While the process of rural development and its impacts, in terms of social and economic change, have been different in different between and within states, the experience of Orissa is worth noting. The dynamics of rural development in the state hardly change the quality of life among marginal groups over period. This is clearly evident from the pattern and trend of growth, employment, poverty, agriculture and infrastructure and social sector development in the state. Off late, other backward states having more or less similar constraints have been able to improve rural life. Therefore, appropriate policy action with special focus on the areas and social groups is suggested to tackle this existing alarming situation. The issue of rural development is more complex and deep rooted and needs specific policy action may be beyond the conventional rural development programmes. The backward districts in southern and northern regions of the state are caught in a vicious circle of multiple deprivation, social exclusion and poor human development. Improvement of social and economic infrastructure in backward regions could be one of top priority to encourage further investment and progress and enhance the capability of the rural poor.

Despite the fact that Orissa confronts with several problems, but the state has the potential to achieve a respectable level of development and to undermine the existing pattern of unequal social and economic pattern among different groups and areas. The key areas for policy actions are correcting structural problems of the economy, accelerating agricultural growth, improving land distribution, investment in infrastructure and human development, good governance, strengthening rural institutions and civil society etc. Agriculture continues to be the mainstay of the people in Orissa but it remains backward, unstable, rain-fed, traditional and prone to natural calamities like drought, flood and cyclone. It appears that agricultural output and growth have been established as major correlates, besides the predominantly rural character of poverty. Productivity of agriculture needs to be improved through better investment in irrigation and technology adoption. Farm and non-farm links to be strengthen in rural areas for productive and sustainable employment for marginal groups. With a view to understand the efficiency of bureaucracy in the economic development in Orissa, present study analysed the development indicators in four different projects in different parts of the state, which was done in terms of four separate case studies. The case studies are:

- Bureaucratic Efficiency in Watershed Programme
- Bureaucratic Efficiency in Joint Forest Management Programme
- Bureaucratic Efficiency in Micro Finance Programme
- Bureaucratic Efficiency in Public Distribution System

## Summary of Findings of the Case Studies

- WHSs as a source of irrigation have positive influence on cropping pattern by means of crop shifting from traditional crops to more valuable cash crops. Perceptible changes are noticed in the yield rate of almost all the crops and the gross return per hectare of land is found satisfactory.

- Adoption of HYV seeds, though moderate, still marginal changes are encouraging. Cropping intensity is not changed because water retaining capacity of WHS is confined to Kharif only.
- During summer, as WHSs are dried up, Rabi crops can't be grown.
- Overall impact of WHS on cropping pattern though encouraging still there is very large scale food insecurity to the extent of 84 percent in the project area and 100 percent in the non-project area.
- It is because of the faulty consumption pattern of the tribals and they are exploited in the product as well as labour market. IWDP Project Implementing Agencies (PIAs) and the NGOs are to be involved for the dedication of liquor among the tribals and beneficiaries in the project area are to be taught on savings in the line of micro finance and grain banks.
- These motivational aspects deserve special attention for the food security of the tribals.
- With the introduction of the JFM program there has been sufficient preservation, protection and maintenance of forest resources, marked improvement in the socio-economic life of the forest fringe households and positive changes in the environmental aspects.
- A fraction of the agricultural labor households have escaped from poverty. Meat and milk production in the VSS areas have increased.
- There has been satisfactory soil and moisture conservation due to the forest protection and forestation activities undertaken by the VSS.
- Added to such benefits, ground water table has improved, forest firing prevented bio-diversity in VSS areas enhanced and occupational mobility improved to a satisfactory level. Effective utilization of MFPs is also reported. People's involvement in the protection of forests is tremendously pro-active.
- However issues like delays in the sanction of funds, non–transparency of the VSS functionaries, insufficient

provision of training and exposure visits for the members have partially hindered the progress.

- Considering that there is tremendous scope for sustainable rural development of the forest fringe households through the JFM program, all types of constraints associated with such type of governance should be removed.
- Simultaneous increase of Plantation crops, horticultural crops, increased milk production, meat production and shifting from traditional crop production to cash crops indicates a good deal of crop diversification which have become possible due to the efforts of the SHGs in watershed areas.
- The households from the lower income groups have improved to higher income. The mean annual household income is calculated to be Rs. 10,450/- against the corresponding figure at Rs. 6175/- during the Pre SHG period.
- It is found that the mean PCPDC of cereals is estimated to be 343.5 Gms during post SHG period which was 296.0 Gms in pre SHG period. Similarly, the mean PCPDC of pulses is found to be 56.6 grams during the post SHG period as against 34.1 grams during the pre-SHG period.
- Micro finance activities through SHGs have significant potential in reducing the incidence of poverty and food insecurity.
- During the post SHG period, only 13 percent of the households are between Rs100-200 as MPCE and about 77 percent between Rs. 200-500 as MPCE. For about 10 percent of the households MPCE has increased to more than Rs. 500.
- Due to increase income consequent upon crop diversification and micro finance activities, conversion of cash into material assets is sufficiently reported in the study area. This indicates increased consumerism and development in rural areas propelled by the forces of micro finance activities.
- Because of the tremendous socio-economic merits

associated with this program, the sustainability of the program is of crucial importance. Convergence of the rural development programs with the micro finance programme could lead to sustainability.

- It is found that around 70 percent of the respondent households in all the blocks under the study are not regularly purchasing from PDS.
- Out of 25 households covered under Antyodaya Anna Yojana, 28.0 % of the households are not lifting their quota regularly. Similarly, around 76 % of the households covered under BPL rice scheme are not regularly lifting their respective PDS quota. Perhaps the comparative lower price of rice under Antyodaya Yojana has encouraged the households to lift their full quota.
- It is revealed that timely non-availability of money is the dominant reason for the irregularity of lifting their quota. Sale, mortgage and gift of ration card is also a major factor for which around 26 % of the beneficiaries are unable to lift their monthly PDS quota.
- In the study area it is reported that many households have sold or mortgaged their ration cards to meet some of their urgent expenses like medical expenses, annual house repair/maintenance and to meet some religious expenses.
- It is understood that around 80 percent of the PDS households, presently, have their ration card. The rest 20% of card holders have either left it with the dealer, sold/mortgaged or lost.
- It is found that in all blocks, majority of households (35%) incur Rs. 60-80 as monthly average expenditure on PDS followed by Rs. 0-20 (25.13%), Rs. 40-60 (14.65%), Rs. 20-40 (12.56%). Around 38% of the households are having monthly average expenditure on PDS in the range of Rs. 0-40 and around 54% of the studied households incur average expenditure of Rs. 0-60 on purchasing rice from PDS in all blocks.
- Due to PDS, only 6.35 percent of households have

escaped from food poverty and 4.86 per cent escaped from income poverty. Thus, the poverty reducing impacts of PDS is very much negligible.

By analyzing the outcome indicators of the various schemes as covered under the cases discussed, the study comes to a conclusion that there is bureaucratic efficiency only in the case of participatory development mode. On the other hand, where development is chiefly under the control of bureaucrats, there is gross inefficiency. In this regard, the Functioning of Public Distribution system is a case in point. Even it is found that motivational aspects of the bureaucracy are not satisfactory.

## Suggestions

- As the responsibility of collectors are enormous, in the interest of the development administration, it would be better if Orissa follows Gujarat and Maharastra pattern of having two separate district heads of development and regulatory administration.
- Old attitudes of bureaucrats should give place to the new in the context of the changing needs of the people. The people friendly attitude must develop.
- A good monitoring and system of execution should develop to get quick and desired result of developmental programmes implemented by the Govt and semi Government agencies.
- Introduction of quality control cell is must for coordination of the ongoing and completed projects.
- There should be specialised training for the elected legislators, councillors and members of panchayat raj System to increase good understanding and capability to handle situation with the bureaucrats. Both the public leaders and the bureaucrats must be dedicated to the cause of public welfare.

# Bibliography

AFC Ltd (2006): "Evaluation Report of DPAP watersheds in Nawarangpur district", Report submitted to Watershed Mission, Bhubaneswar.

Ahluwalia, Montek S. (2000), "Economic Performance of States in Post-Reforms Period", *Economic and Political Weekly,* May 6.

Ahluwalia, Montek S. (2003), "The Economic Performance of the states in the Post-reform period", in *Facets of the Indian Economy,* ed. by Rakesh Mohan, Oxford University Press, New Delhi.

Ahmed, E. (1980): *Bureaucratic Elites in Segmented Economic Growth in Bangladesh and Pakistan,* University Press, Dacca, 1980

Ahmed, L.N. (1975): "New Thinking for Malaysian Public Administration", Dewan Bahasa dan Pustaka, Kuala Lumpur,

Albrow, Martin. 1970. Bureaucracy. London: Pall Mall Press. Originally published in de Grimm, Baron, and Diderot. 1813. Correspondance littéraire, philosophique et critique, 1753-69. 4: 146, 508.

Alogun, M.J,(1983): "Public Administration in Nigeria, A Developmental Approach", Nigeria, Macmillan.

Altekar, A.S., *State and Government in Ancient India,* Benaras, Motilal, Banarsidass, 1955.

Anand, V.E. (1988): "District administration in Orissa: A Reapprisal", in B.B. Jena and J.K. Baral Ed., *Government and Politics in Orissa,* Print House(India), Lucknow, pp. 356-366.

Anderson, G., *British Administration in India,* London, Macmillan, 1917.

Annual Reports of the Commissioner for Scheduled Castes & Scheduled Tribes, Delhi, Manager of Publications.

Annual Reports of the Ministries/Departments of the Government of India.

ASCO, Rayagada, unpublished official Records/Registers.

Augustus, Adebayo (1981): *Principles and Practice of Public Administration in Nigeria,* John Wiley & Sons, Chickester.

B. Pramod and N. Murari Ballal (1992): "Sustainable Development of the Rural Poor", *Pigmy Economic Review,* Vol. 38, No 1.

Bali, J.S. (1990), Integrated Watershed Management: A National Perspective, International Symposium on Water Erosion, Sedimentation and Resource Conservation, October 9-13, Dehradun, India.

Bansal, Hema (2003): "SHG-Bank Linkage Programme in India: An Overview", *Journal of Micro Finance,* Vol. 5, No 1.

Barkam, J.D. and J.J. Okumu (1979): *Politics and Public Policy in Kenya and Tanzania,* New York, Praeger.

Bellamy Carrol (2005): "The State of the World's Children", United Nation's Children's Fund.

Bhambhri, C.P. (1971): *Administrators in a Changing society,* National Publishing House, New delhi

Bhattacharya, B.B. and Arup Mitra (1990), "Excess Growth of Tertiary Sector in Indian Economy: Issues and Implications", *Economic and Political Weekly,* Nov. 3.

Bhol, B.B.; Senapati, P.C. and Dikshit, U.N. (1990), Resource Management in Rainfed watershed: A case study of Munsiguda mini watershed in Phulbani district of Orissa, International symposium on water erosion, sedimentation and resource conservation, Oct. 9-13, Dehradun, India.

Bio-diversity while feeding the world) Financing Agriculture, Oct-Dec.,Vol. 33, No. 4.

Birch, A.H. (1980): *The British System of Government*, London, George Allen & Unwin.

Blondel, Jean (1982): *The Organisation of Governments: A Comparative Analysis of Governmental Structures*, Sage, London, 1982.

Breton, Albert and Ronald Wintrobe (1982): *The Logic of Bureaucratic Conduct*, Cambridge University Press, Cambridge,

Bubach, J.D. et al (1981): *Bureaucrats and Politicians in Western Bureaucracies*, Harvard University Press, Cambridge, 1981.

Caiden, Gerald E. and H. Siedentopp (1982): *Strategies for Administrative Reforms*, Toronto, Heath.

Campbell, George, *India At It May Be London*, John Murray, Albemarle Street, 1853.

Chakrabarti, Rajesh (2006): "The Indian Micro Finance Experience: accomplishments and challenges", in *The financial sector in India- Emerging Issues*, Oxford University press, New Delhi.

"Challenges Ahead – An Overview", *Economic and Political Weekly*, Special Issue on Andhra Pradesh, March 22-29,

"Chhatisgargh & Jharkhand – An Assessment", A project submitted to the International Rice Research Institute, Manila.

Chowdhury, Faizul Latif (2006), *Corrupt Bureaucracy and Privatization of Tax Enforcement*. Dhaka: Pathak Samabesh, ISBN 984-8120-62-9.

Chowdhury, Mustafa (1981): "The Politics of Bureaucracy in Pakistan", Ph.D. Dissertation, York University,

Collins, P. (ed.) (1980): *Administration for Development in Nigeria*, African Education Press, Lagos.

Crozier, M. (1964). *The Bureaucratic Phenomenon* (M. Crozier, Trans). London: Tavistock Publications.

Cuire, Bob (2001): *The Politics of Hunger in India—A Study of Democracy, Governance and Kalahandi's Poverty*, McMillan India Ltd., Chennai.

Curran Lynnc, Nancy Natilson and Robin Young (2006): "Case Study on Profitability of micro finance in commercial Banks: Hatton National Bank", in S. Rajagopalan(Ed), *Micro Finance:*

*Case Studies,* ICFAI University Press, Hyderabad.

Das, B.N. & Pradhan, N.B. (1988): "Political and Economic Development of Orissa", B.B. Jena and J.K. Baral, Ed, *Government and Politics in Orissa,* Print House (India), Lucknow, pp. 42-56.

Dash, C.R. (2007): "Joint Forest Management in Orissa: Some Issues", Working Paper Series, Yojana Ink, No12. /2006 Berhampur.

Datt, Gaurav and Martin Ravallion (2002): 'Is India's Economic Growth Leaving the Poor Behind', World Bank, Policy Research Working Paper.

Dayal, I., Mathur, K. and Bhattacharjya, M. (1976): *District Administration: A Survey for Reorganisation,* McMillan Co., New Delhi.

Deaton, Angus and Dreze, Jean (2002), "Poverty and Inequality in India—A Re-Descriptive Memoirs of the different Ministries", prepared by O&M Division, Cabinet Secretariat.

Dev, M. et al (2003): "Poverty Reduction Strategies in Orissa: Report submitted to PTF Cel", Government of Orissa.

Dev, S. Mahendra (1988): "Regional disparities in Agricultural Labour, Productivity and Rural Labour in India", *The Indian Economic Review,* vol. 23, No.2, July-September.

Dogan, Mattei (ed)(1975): *The Mandarins of Western Europe,* Wiley, New York.

Draper, Hal(1979): "Karl Marx's Theory of Revolution", *State and Bureaucracy,* New York: Monthly Review Press, Vol. 1.

Dudley, B.J.(1982): *An Introduction to Nigerian Government and Politics,* London, Macmillan.

Eldersveld, S.J., A.P. Barnbas and V. Jaganadham (1968): "The Citizen and Administrator in a developing Democracy: An Emipirical Study in Delhi State", Indian Institute of Public Administration, New Delhi.

*Encyclopedia Britannica*. "Bureaucracy". Retrieved June 27, 2007.

Ernest Mandel (1992), *Power and Money: A Marxist Theory of Bureaucracy,* London: Verso, 1992.

Etzioni-Halevy, Eva (1983): *Bureaucracy and Democracy – A Political Dilemma,* Routledge & Kagan Paul, London.

"Examination", *Economic and Political Weekly*, September 7.

FAO (1981): "Forest Resources of Tropical Asia".

Fisek, Kurthan (1970): "On Bureaucracy", *Siyasal Bilgiler Fakultesi Dergisi*, Vol. XXV, No 2, April-June, 1970, Ankara.

Franck, Petiteville (1998):. "Three mythical representations of the state in development theory", *International Social Science Journal*, March 1998 Vol. 50, No. 1.

Gans, J., White, L. D. and Dimmock, M.E. (1986): *The Frontiers of Public Administration*, Chicago University Press.

GoI (1991): "State of Forest Report", Ministry of Environment and Forest, GOI, New Delhi.

GoI (1995): "State of Forest Report", Ministry of Environment and Forest, GOI, New Delhi.

Gole, G.D.H. and Cole Margaret (1984): "A guide to Modern Politics", Victor gollancz.

Goodsell, Charles, T. (1983): *The Case for Bureaucracy: A Public Administration Polemic*, Chatham House Publishers.

Goswami, K.L. (1955): "The Structure of the Development Administration", *Indian Journal of Public Administration*, Vol. 1, No. 2 April-June 1955.

Government of India (2002): "Orissa Development Report", Planning Commission.

Government of Orissa (1996): "Long Term Action Plan for KBK Districts", Planning and Coordination Department.

Government of Orissa (1997): "Socioeconomic Survey of Rural Households", Panchayatiraj Department.

Government of Orissa (2004): "Districts at a Glance", Directorate of Economic and Statistics.

Government of Orissa (2004): Human Development Report, Planning and Coordination Department.

Govt. of India, (2002), National Human Development Report 2001 for India.

Govt. of India, (2002), State Plans, Trends, and Strategies, Tenth Five Year, Plan Volume III.

Govt. of Orissa, (2004), Orissa Human Development Report.

GTZ. BRI (1995): "One Hundred Years Bank Rakyat Indonesia 1895-1995", Jakarta.

Hann Arjan de and Amaresh Dubey (2003): "poverty in orissa: divergent trends with some thoughts on measurement issues", paper presented at NCDS workshops on poverty monitoring, Bhubaneswar.

Hass, D.F. (1979). *Interaction in the Thai Bureaucracy,* Boulder, and West View Press.

Hawkee, Geoffrey (1981): "Who's Master, Who's Servant? : Reforming Bureaucracy", London, George Allen & Unwin.

Heady, Ferrell (1984): "Public Administration: A Comparative Perspective", Marcel, Dekker, New York.

Hirway, I. and B.K. Sahu (2004), *Drought Policy in the Eastern Indian States: Orissa.*

Holley, W.H. and K.M. Jennings (1983): *Personnel Management: Functions and Issues,* The Dryden Press, Chicago.

Huber and Shipan (2002): *Deliberate Discretion: The Institutional Foundations of Bureaucratic Autonomy,* Cambridge University Press, Cambridge.

Hyndman, Patricia (1980): "Constitutional Law and Government", Canberra College of Advanced Education, Belcomen, 1980.

Indira Koneru, e-GOVERNANCE: EMPOWERING CITIZENS THROUGH e-INCLUSION, *ICFAI Journal of Governance and Public Policy,* ICFAI University Press, Hyderabad, September 2008.

Ivan Szelényi, "Social Inequalities in State Socialist Redistributive Economies."

Johnson, Nevil (1973): *Government in the Federal Republic of Germany,* Oxford, Pergamon Press, 1973.

Khan, M.M. and H.M. Zafarullah (ed.)(1980): "Politics and Bureaucracy in a New Nation: Bangladesh", Dacca Centre for Administrative Studies.

Kornaghan, Kenneth (ed.)(1982): *Public Administration in Canada: Selected Readings,* 4th Edition, Methuen, Toronto.

Kropp, Erhard W. and Suran, B.S. (2002): "Linking Banks and (Financial) Self Help Groups in India–An Assessment", Paper presented at the Seminar on SHG-Bank Linkage Programme at New Delhi, Nov. 25-26.

Lee, Hahn-Been and A.C. Samonte (Ed.) (1970): "Administrative Reforms in Asia, Eropa, Menila".

*Legislative Assembly Debates.*

Lowi (1979): *The End of Liberalism*", New York: W. W. Norton & Company.

Ludwig Von Mises (1944): "Bureaucracy".

M.S. Swaminathan Research Foundation (2001), Food Insecurity Atlas in India.

Malhotra, R. (1997): "Incidence of Poverty in India: Towards Consensus on Estimating the Poor", *Indian Journal of Labour Economics,* Vol. 49. No. 1.

Mathur, H.M. (1983): "Training of Development Administrator", APDAC, Kuala Lumpur.

McCubbins and Schwartz. (1984): "Congressional oversight overlooked: Police patrols versus fire alarms", *American Journal of Political Science,* Vol 28

Medina, William A. Changlang (1982): *Bureaucracies: Understanding the Organisation before Selecting the Approach,* Marcel Dekkor, New York.

Merton, Robert K. [1957] 1968. "Bureaucratic Structure and Personality" in *Social Theory and Social Structure,* Glencoe, IL: Free Press. ISBN 0029211301 Retrieved June 27, 2007.

Mohanty, B.B. (2001, 'Land Distribution among Scheduled Castes and Tribes', *Economic and Political Weekly,* October 6.

Murray, D.J. (1978): *Studies in Nigerian Administration* (2nd edition), Hutchinson University Library for Africa, London.

Nachmias, D. and D.H. Rosen Bloom (1980): *Bureaucratic Government,* St. Martin's Press, New York.

Nagaraj, R., Aristomene Varoudakis and Marie-Ange Veganzones (1998), "Long-Run of Reforms", *Economic and Political Weekly,* October 14.

National Wasteland Development Board (1988): "Occurrence of Forest Types in India", Govt. of India, New Delhi.

Neil, Garston (1993): *Bureaucracy: Three Paradigms,* Boston: Kluwer.

Neil, Garston (1993): *Bureaucracy: Three Paradigms,* Boston: Kluwer, 1993.

Norten, E. Long(1952): "Bureaucracy and constitutionalism", *The American Political Science Review,* Vol. XLVI, No. 3, September 1952, pp. 808-818.

Office of the PCCF (2006): "Unpublished Official Records", Govt of Orissa.

Owusu-Ansah, K.A. (1978): "Public Policy Making and the Ghana Civil Service", *Greenhill Journal of Administration,* Vol. 4.

Panda, B.K., Panda, R.K. and Sarangi, P.(2007): Impact of Water Harvesting structures on Dry Land Agriculture in KBK Districts of orissa, *Journal of Rural Development,* NIRD, Hyderabad, June–December.

Panda, B.K. and Panda, R.K. (2007): "Poverty and Level of living among the Tribals in the KBK Districts of Orissa", *Indian Economic Journal.*

Panda, Bijaya Kumar, Radha Krushna Panda and Prasanta Sarangi (2005): "Impact of Water Harvesting Structures on Cropping Pattern and Food Security", *Orissa Economic Journal,* Vol. 36, No. 1 and 2.

Panda, R.K. (2006): "Poverty and Public Distribution System in Orissa with Special Reference to KBK Districts", Unpublished Ph.D. Dissertation submitted to Berhampur University, Orissa.

Panda, R.K. and Das, C.R. (2009): "Joint Forest Management towards Sustainable Rural Development in Orissa", *ICFAI Journal of Governance and Public Policy,* March.

Panda, R.K., J.N. Panda (2007): "Socio Economic and Environmental Changes and Joint Forest Management" in S.N. Tripathy(Ed), *Dynamics of Rural Development,* Discovery Publishing House, New Delhi.

Panda, R.K. and K.C. Patnaik (2007): "Functioning of Joint Forest Management in Orissa", Working Paper Series, No. 11./ 2006, Yojana Ink, Berhampur.

Panda, M. (2002), 'Poverty in Orissa: A Disaggregated Analysis', paper for the NCCDS workshop on poverty monitoring, Bhubaneswar, February.

Paul H. Appleby, *Public Administration in India: Report of a Survey;* Cabinet Secretariat, Delhi, Manager of Publications, 1957.

Peagels, Carl (1984): *Japan Vs the West*, Kluwer, Boston.

Personnel Offices Association of the Philippines (1976): "Handbook of Information on the Philippine Civil Service", Phoenix Press, Quezon City, 1976.

Petiteville, Frank (1998): "Three Mythical Representatives of the state in development Theory", *International Social Science Journal*, March, Vol. 50, No. 1.

Pitschas, Rainer (1993): "Aspects of Max Weber's Theory on Bureaucracy and New public management Approach", *The Indian Journal of Public Administration,* Vol. 39, No. 4.

Planning Commission (1977): "Sixth Five Year Plan Technical Note", Govt. of India.

Planning Commission (1993), The Task Force on projections of Minimum needs and Effective consumption demand.

Planning Commission (2002): "Orissa Development Report", Govt of India.

Poudyal, M.P. (1984): "Public Administration and Nation Building in Nepal", NBO, Delhi.

Pradhan, Jagdish (2002): "Causes of Hunger and Starvation Deaths in the Tribal Areas of KBK Region and How this problem could be tackled", Mimeographed, Sahabhagi Vikas Abhiyan, Bhubaneswar.

Pradhan, N. B. (2005): "A Political Economy of Tribal People, Minerals and Forest in Orissa", Keynote Address at a National Seminar held at the P. G. Department of Economics, Berhampur University, 27th April.

Pradhan, N.B. (2005): "Dynamics of Poverty and Underdevelopment in Orissa, Presidential Address, 37th Annual Conference of Orissa Economic Association held at Christ College, Cuttack, 19-20, February 2005.

Price, Robe M. (1975): *Society and Bureaucracy in Contemporary Ghana*, University of California Press, Berkeley.

Quah, S.T. (1978): "Administrative and Legal Measures for Combating Bureaucratic Corruption in Singapore", Occasional Paper No. 34, Department of Political Science, University of Singapore.

R. Radhakrishna, S. Indrakant, C. Ravi (2004): "Changing Food Preferences, Nutritional Intake and Nutritional Status" in

Aditya Bhatacharjee (eds.), *Globalisation and the Developing Economies: Theory and Evidence,* Center for Economic and Social Studies.

R. Radhakrishna and C. Ravi (2004): "Malnutrition in India: Trends and Determinants", *Economic and Political Weekly,* Vol. 3, No. 7

R. Radhakrishna and Shovan Roy (2004): "Poverty in India Dimensions and Character" in Kirit Parikh and R. Radhakrishna (eds.), *India Development Report,* Oxford University Press.

Radin, B.A. (2007): "The Indian Administrative Service (IAS) in the 21 stCentury: Living in an Intergovernmental Environment", *International Journal of Public Administration,* Vol. 30, No. 12.

Rajgopalan, S. (2006): *Micro Finance: Case Studies,* ICFAI University Press, Hyderabad.

Raksasataya Amara and Hemrich Siedentope (ed.) (1980): "Asian Civil Services Developments and Trends", Apdac, Kuala Lumpur.

Ramseyer and Rosenbluth.(1993): *Japan's Political Marketplace,* Cambridge: Harvard University Press.

Rao, N. Prahallad (1994): "Nutrition" in NIPCCD (eds.), *Child in India: A Statistical Profile,* New Delhi.

Rao, C.H. Hanumantha and S. Mahendra Dev (2003), "Economic Reforms and

Rao, M. Govinda, R.T. Shand and K.P. Kalirajan (1999), "Convergence of Incomes Across Indian States – A Divergent View", *Economic and Political Weekly,* March 27.

Rao, M.S. Ramamohan, Chittaranjan S. and Singh Gurmel (1990), Soil and water conservation measures for Red and Black soils of Semi Arid Region of South India, International Symposium on Water Erosion, Sedimentation and Resource Conservation, Oct. 9-13, Dehradun, India.

Rath, Sharadini, 2003, 'Productivity and Food Security: A Marginal Situation Case Study', Centre for Budget and Policy Studies,

RCDC, 1999, Development Innovators, 'Impact of Deforestation on Socio-Economic Conditions of Tribal Communities in Orissa', Bhubaneswar,

RCDC, 2000, 'Social and Institutional Analysis and Livelihood Systems Study of Tribal Communities in Selected Villages in Kandhamal and Gajapati Districts', Bhubaneswar.

Report of the Direct Taxes Administration Enquiry Committee, 1958-59, Ministry of Finance, Delhi, Manager of Publications, 1960.

Report of the Committee on Ministers' Powers, cmd.4060, London, H.M.S.O. 1932.

Report of the Committee on the Management and Control of Research and Development, London, H.M.S.O., 1961

Report of the Committees of the Panel on Land Reform, New Delhi, Planning Commission, 1959.

Report of the Customs Re-organisation Committee, 1957-58, Ministry of Finance, Delhi, Manager of Publications, 1959.

Report of the East India Railway Committee (Acworth Committee), 1020-21.

Report of the Health Survey & Development Committee, Delhi, Manager of Publications, 1946.

Report of the Indian Jails Committee, Government of India, 1919-20.

Report of the Joint Committee on Indian Constitutional Reform, London, H.M.S.O., 1934.

Report of the Joint Select Committee of the House of Lords and the House of Commons on the Government of India Act, 1919, Calcutta, Central Publication Branch, 1924.

Report of the Railway Corruption Enquiry Committee, 1953-55, Ministry of Railways, Delhi Manager of Publications, 1961.

Report of the Royal Commission upon Decentralization, 1907-9.

Report of the Sanskrit Commission, 1956-57, Ministry of Education, Delhi, Manager of Publications, 1958.

Report of the Seamen's Recruitment Committee, Government of India, 1922.

Report of the Secretariat Procedure Committee, Government of India, 1920.

Report of the States Reorganisation Commission, 1953-55, Delhi, Manager of Publications, 1955.

Report of the Working of the System of Government, United Provinces of Agra and Oudh, 1921-26, Allahabad, 1930.

Report on Indian Constitutional Reforms, Simla, Government of India Press, 1918.

Report on the Working of the Reformed Constitution, 1927, Calcutta, Central Publication Branch, 1928.

Robin Jack, et a1 (ed.)(1984): "Managing Administration", Marcel Dekker, New York.

Sahu B. K.( 2003): 'Access to Land, Land Markets and Poverty: Re-emerged Policy Option; Some Emerging Trends in Orissa–A Review' in D.N. Reddy (ed.) *Land market and Poverty,* CRS, LBSNAA, Musorrie

Sahu, B.K. 2003, "Growth of Non-farm sector in backward agriculture: A study of three region in Orissa', a paper presented in the national seminar on Non-Farm Employment, NIRD, Hyderabad

Sahu, Basant Kumar (1997): "Poverty, Anti-Poverty Programmes and Rural Change: A Study of Selected Tribal Villages in Phulbani", Unpublished Ph. D. Thesis submitted to Berhampur University.

Sahu P. (2003) "Post-reform rural employment scenario in Orissa", in K. Sarap (eds.) *Agrarian Transformation in Orissa,* Sambalpur University.

Sarap, K. 1998. "On the Operation of the Land Market in Backward Agriculture: Evidence form a Village in Orissa, Eastern India", *Journal of Peasant Studies* 25(2): 102-30.

Saxena, Rakesh (2004): "Governance of Forest resources in India: A brief review and Identification of Current Issues", Paper presented at Eastern Zone Reflective Workshop on Governance: Gender, Poverty and Livelihood, held at NCDS, Bhubaneswar, 20-21 July.

Scholz and Wood (1988): "Controlling the IRS: Principals, Principles, and Public Administration", *American Journal of Political Science,* Vol. 42 (January).

Second Report of the Reconstruction Committee on Reconstruction Planning, Delhi, Manager of Publications, 1944.

Seibel, Hans and Dave, H.R. (2002): "Commercial Aspects of SHG Banking in India", Paper presented at the Seminar on SHG-Bank Linkage Programme at New Delhi, Nov. 25-26

Sghaffer, Bernard (ed.)(1974): *Administrative Training and Development: A Comparative Study of East Africa, Zambia Pakistan and India,* New York, Praeger, 1974.

Shah, Amita and Guru Baidyanath (2003), Poverty in remote rural areas in India: A Review of Evidence and Issues, Gujurat Institute of Development Research, Working paper No. 139.

Shand, Ric and S. Bhide (2000), "Sources of Economic Growth–Regional Dimensions".

Sharma, Devinder (2003), Bio-tech age: From Hunger to Hidden Hunger, *Financing Agriculture,* Vol. 35, No. 4.

Sharma, Manohar P. (2006): "Community Driven Development and Scaling up of micro finance Services: Case Studies from Nepal and India", in S. Rajagopalan(Ed), *Micro Finance: Case Studies,* ICFAI University Press, Hyderabad.

Shiva, Vandana (2003): Having our Cake and Eating it too.

Singh, Gurmel (1990), Rain water Harvesting and Recycling For Sustainable Agricultural Production, International Symposium on water erosion, Sedimentation and Resource conservation, Oct. 9-13, Dehradun, India.

Singh, N.K. (1974): *Bureaucracy: Positions and Persons,* Abhinav Publications, New Delhi.

Sivanappan, R.K. (2004). "Water Harvesting and conservation in Dry .land on watershed basis", *Financing Agriculture,* Vol. 36, No. 4.

Subramaniam, V. (1967): "Role of Civil service in Indian political system", *The Indian Journal of Public Administration,* Vol. XVII, No. 2, April-June 1967.

Summary of Proceedings of the Import Advisory Council.

Summary of Proceedings of the National Railway Users' Consultative Council, Ministry of Railways.

The Organization for Women and Rural Development (2002): "Functioning of Women Self Help Groups in Orissa". Report submitted to Department of Women and Child Development, Govt. of India, New Delhi.

Tripathy, A.K. (1988): "Inter Departmental Cooperation at District level in Orissa" in B.B. Jena and J.K. Baral Ed., *Government and politics in Orissa,* Print House(India), Lucknow, pp. 345-355.

Vittal, N. (2003), *Corruption in India: The Roadblock to National Prosperity,* Academic Foundation,

Watson, N.; Deeming, H. and Treffny, R. (2009): "Beyond bureaucracy? Assessing institutional change in the governance of water in England", *Water Alternatives* Vol. 2, No. 3.

Watson, Tony J. (1980). *Sociology, Work and Industry*. Routledge, ISBN 0-415-32165-4.

Watson, Tony J. (1980): *Sociology, Work and Industry,* Routledge, ISBN 0-415-32165-4.

Watson, Tony J. 1980, *Sociology, Work and Industry,* Routledge, ISBN 0415321654.

Weber, Max. [1947] 1997. *The Theory of Social and Economic Organization,* Free Press.

Wilensky, H.L. (1975). *The Welfare State and Equality,* University of California Press, Berkeley. .

Williams, G. (1980): *State and Society in Nigeria,* Afrografika Publishers, Idonre.

Wiswawarnapala, W.A. (1974): "Civil Service Administration in Ceylon", 1974.

Woodrow Wilson (1887): "The Study of Administration" *Political Science Quarterly,* Vol. 2, No. 2, June.

Wright, Edward Reynolds (ed.) (1976): *Korean Politics in Transition,* University of Washington, Press, Seattle.

# Index